To all the readers and learners.

Contents

API VIGILANCE MULESOFT MONITORING STRATEGIES

A Complete Handbook on MuleSoft API Monitoring

AJAY PRATAP SINGH
ASHISH KHATARKAR

Copyright © 2025 AJAY PRATAP SINGH, ASHISH KHATARKAR

All Rights Reserved.

This book has been self-published with all reasonable efforts taken to make the material error-free by the author. No part of this book shall be used, reproduced in any manner whatsoever without written permission from the author, except in the case of brief quotations embodied in critical articles and reviews.

The Author of this book is solely responsible and liable for its content including but not limited to the views, representations, descriptions, statements, information, opinions and references ["Content"]. The Content of this book shall not constitute or be construed or deemed to reflect the opinion or expression of the Publisher or Editor. Neither the Publisher nor Editor endorse or approve the Content of this book or guarantee the reliability, accuracy or completeness of the Content published herein and do not make any representations or warranties of any kind, express or implied, including but not limited to the implied warranties of merchantability, fitness for a particular purpose. The Publisher and Editor shall not be liable whatsoever for any errors, omissions, whether such errors or omissions result from negligence, accident, or any other cause or claims for loss or damages of any kind, including without limitation, indirect or consequential loss or damage arising out of use, inability to use, or about the reliability, accuracy or sufficiency of the information contained in this book.

Made with ♥ on the Notion Press Platform

www.notionpress.com

About The Authors

AJAY PRATAP SINGH is Lead Integration Architect at IBM and has over 19 years of expertise in Enterprise Application Integration (EAI), He is a highly accomplished Integration Architect. He is an **Open Group Certified Technical Specialist**, **AWS Certified Architect** and **MuleSoft Certified Integration Architect**. His deep technical knowledge and hands-on experience make him a key player in designing, implementing, and optimizing integration solutions across diverse industries.

As a technology enthusiast, he specializes in multi-cloud and hybrid integration scenarios, ensuring seamless interoperability between on-premises and cloud environments. He has successfully led numerous implementation, re-implementation, transformation, and migration projects, delivering robust and scalable integration architectures tailored to business needs.

ASHISH KHATARKAR is Integration Architect at IBM. He is an accomplished Integration Architect with over 19 years of experience in software development and integration across various technologies. He is currently working as an Integration Architect at IBM India. Throughout his career, he has held key roles at leading companies such as Capgemini, TCS, and Reliance.

Ashish holds a Master of Technology (M.Tech) along with multiple certifications include a MuleSoft **Certified Integration Architect** and an **AWS Certified** . His expertise lies in **Enterprise Application Integration (EAI)**, with a strong background in designing and managing large-scale application implementations, upgrades, and integration project migrations. With his extensive experience in middleware and application services architecture, Ashish continues to deliver impactful integration solutions for global enterprises.

Foreword

In today's interconnected digital landscape, APIs serve as the backbone of modern applications, enabling seamless data exchange, system interoperability and serve as glue binding complex enterprise ecosystems together. With businesses increasingly relying on APIs to deliver critical services, ensuring their performance, reliability, and security is more important than ever. Also, as APIs scale in volume and complexity, API monitoring/observability becomes a strategic enabler for organizations.

I have been working with many clients in their API transformational journeys over the last few years. Being a thought leader in Enterprise application integration and with more than 25 years of experience in IT industry, I have led large programs in data and API integrations for clients across industries. Over the course of my career working with MuleSoft implementations across various industries, I have seen the transformative impact that a well-structured monitoring approach can have.

I've seen firsthand how API monitoring, when implemented thoughtfully, can mean the difference between minutes and hours of downtime, between proactive insights and reactive scrambling. Yet, despite its importance, monitoring is often treated as an afterthought. That's why this book is such a timely and valuable resource, especially when enterprises are witnessing API sprawl.

Effective API monitoring goes beyond just detecting failures—it provides insights that help organizations proactively prevent issues, optimize performance, and power customer experience.

This book offers deep dive into the world of API monitoring and management with MuleSoft. It delves into both proactive and reactive monitoring strategies for tracking API health, performance, security and equips the teams to design systems that are inherently observable.

From exploring powerful capabilities of the Anypoint Platform's native monitoring tools to integrating with external solutions to create robust end to end observability, this book provides the knowledge and context needed to elevate any MuleSoft deployment.

Whether you are a developer, API architect, or operations specialist, this book will equip you with the knowledge and strategies needed to establish an effective API monitoring practice that ensures system resilience and business continuity.

What makes this guide truly stand out is its practical focus with real world experience and thoughtful insights. Rather than just presenting monitoring as theoretical discipline, it offers practical guidance. Whether you're a developer fine-tuning performance, an architect designing resilient systems, or part of a DevOps team responsible for uptime, you'll find actionable insights tailored to real-world challenges.

It's not just about dashboards and alerts—it's about building confidence in your APIs and ensuring they can deliver under pressure. Readers will gain a clear understanding of how to track API health, performance, usage trends, and potential vulnerabilities—insights that are critical to maintaining resilient, high-performing systems.

I commend the authors for bringing much-needed clarity to such a critical area of MuleSoft operations. I encourage you to not only read and apply what you learn, challenge your current monitoring approaches, and embrace observability as a core part of your API lifecycle. Consider how the strategies and best practices outlined in this book can help you build observable, trustworthy and sustainable systems.

Cheers,

Jyoti Patil

Pune, India

Preface

In today's digital economy, the seamless integration of systems, applications, and data is crucial for the success of any enterprise. MuleSoft, as a leading integration platform, has empowered organizations to connect their applications, data, and devices with unprecedented speed and agility. However, with great power comes great responsibility, and as businesses increasingly rely on interconnected ecosystems, the importance of robust monitoring and management of these integrations cannot be overstated.

This book is a comprehensive guide to MuleSoft monitoring, designed for integration architects, developers, operations teams, and IT leaders who are tasked with ensuring the smooth functioning of their MuleSoft environments. Whether you are a seasoned MuleSoft professional or new to the platform, this book will provide you with the insights, strategies, and tools needed to effectively monitor, manage, and optimize your MuleSoft integrations.We will explore the full spectrum of MuleSoft monitoring, from the basics of setting up monitoring dashboards to advanced techniques for proactive monitoring and anomaly detection. You will learn how to leverage MuleSoft's built-in monitoring tools, as well as integrate third-party solutions to create a comprehensive monitoring strategy. Additionally, we will delve into best practices for setting up alerts, analyzing logs, and ensuring compliance with enterprise governance standards using policies.

The journey through this book is intended to be practical and hands-on, with real-world examples and scenarios that you are likely to encounter in your own integration projects. The goal is to equip you with the knowledge and confidence to not only keep your MuleSoft integrations running smoothly but to anticipate and prevent potential issues before they impact your business.

Monitoring is not just about reacting to problems; it's about building a resilient and adaptive integration environment that supports your business goals. By the end of this book, you will have a deep understanding of how to achieve this with MuleSoft, ensuring that your integrations are not only efficient but also resilient, secure, and future proof. We will also touch upon use of Generative AI and Agentic AI in building a resilient and adaptive integration environment.

Thank you for embarking on this journey with us. We hope that this book becomes a valuable resource in your MuleSoft monitoring endeavors, helping you to build and maintain a robust integration landscape that drives success for your organization.

Chapter 1: API Monitoring This chapter introduces the concept of monitoring, explaining what it is, why it is essential. It also covers the key aspects that make monitoring effective. By the end of this chapter, readers will understand importance of monitoring in today's digital world, impact on business if monitoring is not in place and how it helps businesses maintain continuity with minimal interruptions.

Chapter 2: Anypoint Platform Monitoring This chapter explores the various types of monitoring available, providing a detailed examination of both proactive and reactive approaches to ensure optimal system performance and issue resolution.

Chapter 3: Anypoint Platform Monitoring This chapter explores the various monitoring features available in MuleSoft's Anypoint Platform. It covers how to enable these features, different types of alerts, and step-by-step process for setting up alerts. Additionally, it discusses the logging capabilities, in-built

& custom dashboard. Numerours use cases are provided for various alerts. This can help reader making decision on alert setup scenarios. You will acquire a comprehensive understanding of how to effectively monitor and manage MuleSoft Applications/API using Anypoint Platform Monitoring.

Chapter 4: External Monitoring Tools This chapter introduces external monitoring tools, explaining the various options available and how they can be integrated with MuleSoft Applications/APIs across different deployment models. It provides a step-by-step guide on the integration process, offering practical insights into using these tools for enhanced monitoring and management. By the end of this chapter, readers will understand how to leverage external tools to ensure the effective performance and reliability of their MuleSoft Applications/APIs.

Chapter 5: Shift Left Approach in Monitoring Management This chapter explores the shift-left approach for API monitoring solution, explaining its key principles, benefits, and practical use cases. It also covers, how to build intelligence in CICD pipeline to avoid API monitoring configurations after go-live in production. This chapter will give you clear understanding of how adopting a shift-left approach can improve system reliability and proactively address potential issues.

Chapter 6: Monitoring Strategy and Best Practices This chapter focuses on developing an effective monitoring strategy and outlines the best practices to follow for maintaining system performance and reliability. It provides actionable insights to help you design a robust monitoring framework, ensuring early detection of issues and minimizing downtime.

Chapter 7: AIOps & API Observability This chapter explores AIOps and its key features, implementation roadmap, and the transformative role of Generative and Agentic AI in elevating API monitoring and management.

Chapter 8: Real World Examples This chapter highlights various real-world use cases that provide valuable insights for designing effective monitoring solutions.

Acknowledgments

With deep gratitude and reverence, I extend my heartfelt thanks to Shri Om Swami Ji, whose divine blessings have been a guiding light throughout my journey. His wisdom and spiritual presence have provided me with the strength and clarity needed to bring this book to life.

I also wish to express my sincere appreciation for the vast reservoirs of knowledge available on the internet, which have served as invaluable resources in shaping my understanding. A special thanks to my family for their unwavering moral support, patience, and encouragement, which kept me motivated at every step.

- AJAY PRATAP SINGH

With profound gratitude, I extend my heartfelt thanks to my family. Your unwavering support and endless encouragement have been the bedrock of my strength. Through every challenge and triumph, your belief in me never wavered. I am blessed to have you as my constant source of inspiration and love.

I also wish to express my appreciation to the leaders and colleagues who have inspired and supported me. Your dedication and vision have been a source of motivation, and I am privileged to have learned from each of you. Your leadership has shaped my perspective and strengthened my resolve. Big thanks to Jyoti Patil and Ajay Pratap Singh (co-authors) .

- ASHISH KHATARKAR

Who Should Read This Book?

The audience for this book on MuleSoft API monitoring would primarily include:

- **Integration Architects:** Professionals responsible for planning and architecting Integration Solution within their organizations. These individuals are responsible for identifying and incorporating Monitoring and management requirement in the solution design.
- **Developers and Engineers:** Those who work with MuleSoft Anypoint Platform and are involved in designing, implementing, and maintaining APIs. Those who are part of C4E (Center for Enablement Team) or Platform Engineering Team.
- **DevOps Engineers:** Individuals involved designing and implementing CICD pipeline and involved in deploying, scaling, and managing API infrastructure, who need to ensure the reliability and performance of APIs in production environments.
- **Integration Support Engineers:** Those tasked with configuring and managing the monitoring tools and infrastructure necessary for tracking API performance and health.
- **Technical Managers and Decision Makers:** Leaders responsible for making strategic decisions about API initiatives within their organizations, who need to understand the importance of monitoring and how it impacts business objectives. This book gives an insight about monitoring features and Business Analyst, Technical Managers can consider these features at the time of requirement gathering.
- **Students and Researchers:** Those studying or researching API management, integration technologies, or related fields who are looking to deepen their understanding of API monitoring best practices.

Prologue

This book is about various approaches and methods for monitoring of MuleSoft Application/APIs in a proactive and reactive way. Monitoring can be broadly done at three levels:

- Application/API-level monitoring
- Network-level monitoring
- Platform-level monitoring

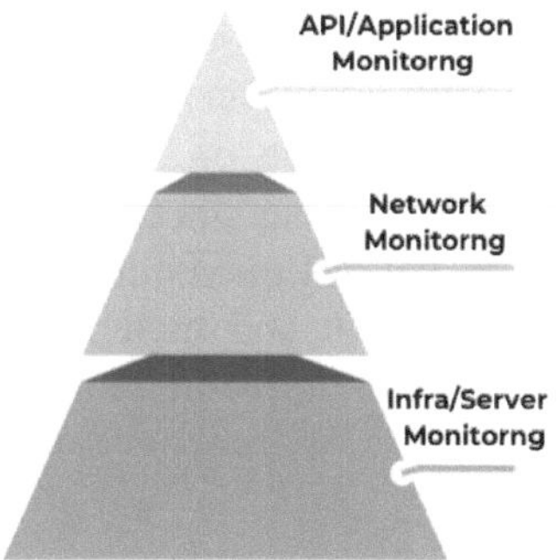

Figure 1 - Monitoring Level

- **Infrastructure/Platform Monitoring:** It is commonly known as server monitoring, involves tracking server resources to ensure optimal performance and reliability. Key metrics such as CPU utilization, memory usage, and disk space are continuously observed to detect potential issues, prevent downtime, and maintain system efficiency.
- **Network Monitoring:** It is about tracking requests and responses across network components, including switches, firewalls, and servers, ensures seamless

communication and performance. This monitoring helps detect bottlenecks, security threats, and potential failures, enabling proactive troubleshooting and maintaining network reliability.

- **API/Application Monitoring:** Application monitoring plays a vital role in assessing the overall performance of a service. It helps track key metrics, detect inefficiencies, and ensure that applications operate smoothly. By continuously evaluating performance, organizations can maintain optimal service levels and prevent potential disruptions.

Scope of this book is **Application/API level monitoring**. It includes various methods and tools for continuously observing your APIs, checking their performance, spotting any hiccups or errors and letting you know if anything needs attention.We have observed there are ample of books on Architecture, Design and Development of APIs. However, I didn't find specific book on Monitoring & Management of APIs deployed in MuleSoft Anypoint Platform. This is our sincere effort to bring this book for you so that you can harvest maximum benefit out of it. You can contemplate the approach and methods provided in this book while designing APIs or implementing monitoring solution for your API network.

1. API Monitoring

What is API Monitoring?

API Monitoring in general refers to the process of observing and managing performance, availability, and behavior of APIs over time. The primary goal of monitoring is to ensure that these APIs and integrated systems operate as expected, meet performance targets, and remain available to end users. Monitoring of APIs enables us to identify problems and resolve it in a timely manner. This type of problems can arise due to following reasons:

Functional Error Arising Due to Improper Data

This happens when a data is sent from source is not fitting in the processing logic of end system or a particular data is not configured in end system. Due to this anomaly, end system returns failure response. For example, source system is sending address change for a customer in billing system. However, the customer is not yet provisioned in the billing system. In this case, Billing system will always return a functional error response, stating that customer not found. This may eventually get converted to an incident.

Master Data Discrepancy in Source and Target Systems

This is a case when master data is not updated in the end system. We can understand from example of Billing System API and Billing Experience API. There are new plan master data created in the master data management system and plan is rolled out to market. Now due to XYZ reason, this plan master data is not replicated to Billing System. In this case, any plan change request for a customer will fail. Billing system will not be able to translate the plan found in the request payload.

Discrepancy of Releases Among Systems

This happens when accidently wrong releases moved to production. This can be a case where either source system deployed next version before compatible MuleSoft API version is moved to production. Another case might be where target system release was deployed in siloes and Integration team was not informed/notified, or it was not aligned with the corresponding API release.

Resource utilization is crossing threshold limit

This can be a case where allocated CPU and Memory utilization of APIs are breaching the threshold limit.

Calls between APIs Layers are Timing Out

In any integration solution we have source, integration layer (API) and end system. We have two points of timeout failure in the simplest integration via API. First point of timeout failure can be observed due to end system not responding in expected time interval. Second point of timeout failure can be observed due to API is overwhelmed with number of request and not able to respond or process the request from source system. This results in a timeout error. This is depicted in the diagram below:

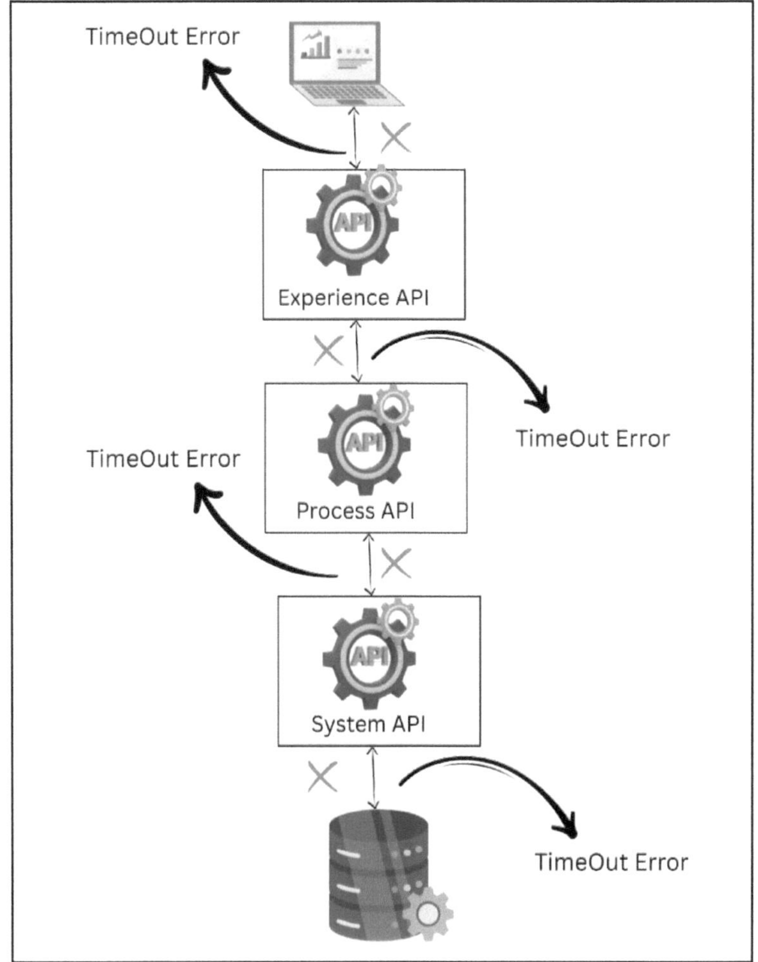

Figure 1.1 - Timeout Error

Policy Enforcement Violation

Error may occur due to policy voilation. There migh multiple such cases as per your list of policies applied on MuleSoft API. Lets understand this with few examples:

- **Rate Limiting Policy:** If ingress request is more than numbers defined in the rate limit policies, it can result in error.

- **Strict container depth for JSON threat protection:** If the container depth or string value for the field is not conforming to the values coming the request payload, it will result in error.

Network issues

Error occurring due to firewall port, IP whitelisting, DNS resolution.

Credentials expired

Error occurring due to expired credentials such as user, password, role id etc.

SSL certificates expired

When the certificate used in the API code expires, it triggers an authentication failure, preventing secure communication between systems. This can result in the API being unable to establish a trusted connection, leading to errors when processing requests.

Such certificate expirations, can cause significant disruptions in API functionality, affecting dependent services and user experiences. To prevent this, it is essential to implement proactive monitoring and automated alerts for certificate validity, ensuring timely renewal and uninterrupted API performance.

Why API Monitoring is important?

API monitoring plays a critical role in ensuring the reliability, availability, and performance of APIs and integrated data sources. Monitoring of APIs supports proactive management, problem resolution, and optimization efforts.

APIs in siloes are good for nothing. In modern architecture all the enterprise and legacy applications in an enterprise are integrated via APIs. All the enterprise and legacy applications expose their data and functionality via APIs. API based modern integration architecture is depicted in the following diagram.

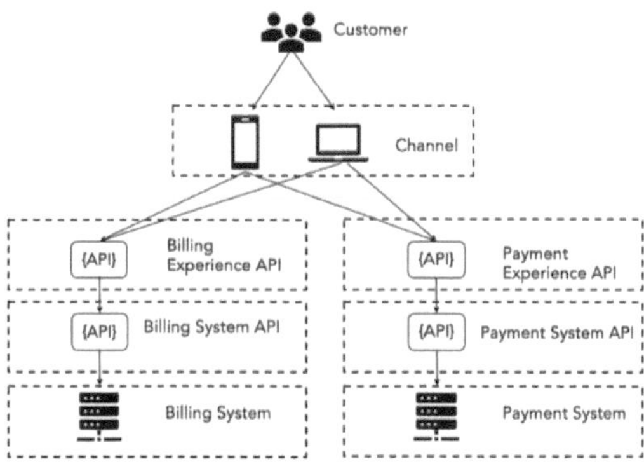

Figure 1.2 - API Led Integration Architecture

Above diagram shows high level architecture of Business Support Systems integrated via APIs. We can see, there are four APIs which are involved in this integration. Two APIs are south bound system specific APIs which are exposing the billing system functionalities and payment system functionalities. The other two APIs are customer facing APIs which are consumed via channel application (e.g. mobile app, web application etc.).

In this example, customer can query their bill amount via customer facing billing API which further consumes API exposing billing system feature. This API at the end interacts with billing system.Similarly, payment APIs are meant for posting payment or querying payment status. There might be many failure points in this design. Any connection failure between the components will result a functional impact. There will be financial impact, if payment APIs are not working. If billing APIs are not working customer will not be able to see billed amount or unbilled amount. Even customer will not be able to change his data or call plan. This will lead to customer dissatisfaction and may lead to customer churn. Hence, if monitoring of APIs is not in place, any problem occurring in production may impact customer significantly as shown in the image.

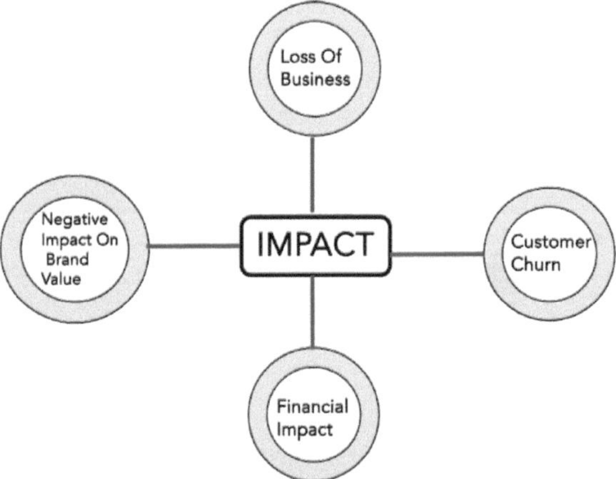

Figure 1.3 - Impact on Business

Monitoring is essential for ensuring the reliability, availability, performance, security, and cost-effectiveness of your IT systems and services. It enables proactive management, problem resolution, and optimization, ultimately contributing to the success of your organization.

Monitoring and It's Key Aspects

Monitoring involves the following key aspects:

Data collection

Monitoring systems collect various types of data, including performance metrics, logs, events, and traces, from the monitored components. This data provides insights into the health, status, and behavior of the systems and helps identify issues or anomalies.

Metrics and KPIs

Monitoring involves tracking and analyzing key performance indicators (KPIs) and metrics relevant to the monitored systems or services. These metrics may include response times, error rates, throughput, CPU utilization, memory usage, network latency, and more.

Alerting and Notification

Monitoring systems typically include alerting mechanisms to notify administrators or support engineers about critical events, anomalies, or deviations from normal behavior. Alerts can be configured based on predefined thresholds or conditions to prompt timely action and problem resolution. Precondition thresholds are identified as part of requirement collection.

Visualization and Reporting

Monitoring data is often visualized using dashboards, charts, graphs, or reports to provide stakeholders with a clear and intuitive understanding of system performance and health. Visualization tools help identify trends, patterns, and correlations in the data.

Analysis and Troubleshooting

Monitoring data is analyzed to identify root causes of issues, diagnose problems, and optimize system performance. Analysis techniques may involve correlation, anomaly detection, trend analysis, and statistical methods to gain actionable insights from the collected data.

Continuous Improvement

Monitoring is an iterative process aimed at continuously improving the reliability, performance, and efficiency of systems and services. Feedback from monitoring data helps drive optimization efforts, capacity planning, and infrastructure investments to meet evolving requirements and challenges

Monitoring of APIs Helps in Many Ways

Early Detection of Issues

Monitoring allows to detect issues and anomalies in integration landscape or API behavior early, before they escalate into major incidents. Early detection enables prompt intervention and reduces the impact on users and operations.

Ensuring Reliability and Availability

Monitoring helps ensure that your APIs are available and accessible to users when needed. By tracking availability metrics and detecting downtime or service interruptions, you can minimize service disruptions and maintain high reliability.

Optimizing Performance

Monitoring provides insights into the performance of your APIs and integration business processes, allowing you to identify performance bottlenecks, optimize resource utilization, and improve responsiveness. By analyzing performance metrics, you can enhance user experience and meet performance targets.

Capacity Planning and Scalability

Monitoring helps you understand resource usage patterns and forecast future resource requirements. This information is crucial for capacity planning and scaling your infrastructure to accommodate growing demand or changing workloads effectively.

Security and Compliance

Monitoring enables you to detect security threats, unauthorized access attempts, and suspicious activities in your systems or networks. By monitoring for security events and compliance violations, you can mitigate risks, enforce security policies, and maintain regulatory compliance.

Cost Optimization

Monitoring helps optimize resource utilization and control operational costs. By identifying inefficiencies, over-provisioned resources, and idle capacity, you can optimize resource allocation, minimize waste, and reduce infrastructure expenses.

Continuous Improvement

Monitoring provides feedback on the performance and health of your systems, enabling continuous improvement and optimization efforts. By analyzing monitoring data and identifying areas for improvement, you can enhance system reliability, performance, and efficiency over time.

2. Exploring Different Flavours of Monitoring

An ounce of prevention is worth a pound of cure. — Benjamin Franklin

API monitoring can be approached reactively or proactively. A reactive approach involves addressing issues like downtime, slow response times, or errors after they occur, often based on user complaints or post-incident alerts. While it has lower initial costs, it risks user dissatisfaction, SLA breaches, and higher long-term costs due to frequent firefighting. In contrast, a proactive approach focuses on real-time monitoring, anomaly detection, and predictive analytics to identify and prevent issues before they impact users. Though it requires a higher upfront investment, it ensures better reliability, compliance with SLAs, and minimal user impact, making it crucial for business-critical APIs. Let's understand this in more details:

Proactive Monitoring:

Proactive monitoring is akin to wearing smart watch and monitoring heart rate, sleep pattern etc. Or periodically getting preventive health checkup done. This helps in identifying any anomalies observed in the results. Every individual can take advantage of it and immediately consult a doctor if any anomaly is observed. Doctor can corelate the abnormalities and take action to treat it before it gets converted to critical illness.

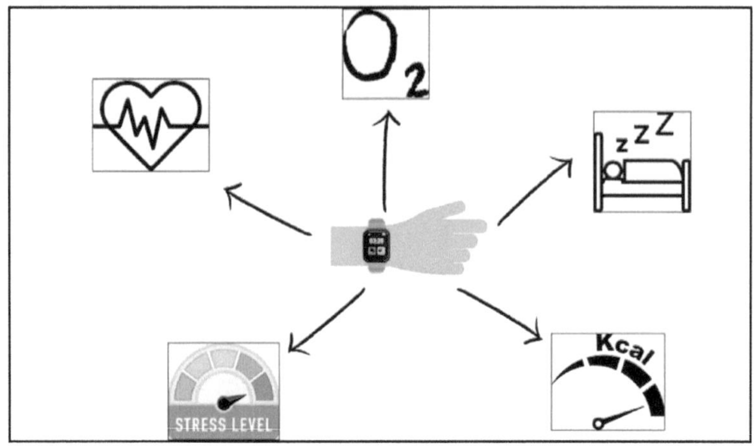

Figure 2.1 - Proactive Health Monitoring

Like human health, proactive monitoring for api continuously observing the performance, availability, and security of APIs to detect potential issues early and prevent them from impacting users or applications. It focuses on preventing downtime, failures, or performance degradation by continuously monitoring systems and taking preventive actions. This approach ensures APIs remain reliable and performant by identifying potential bottlenecks, security vulnerabilities, or unexpected behavior before they lead to failures or downtime.

Key Characteristics:

- **Preventive:** Proactive monitoring aims to prevent issues before they occur.
- **Continuous:** It involves real-time or regular monitoring of apis and metrices.
- **Predictive:** It uses data analysis, trends, and alerts to predict potential failures.
- **Automation:** Often relies on automated tools to detect anomalies and trigger alerts.

Examples of proactive monitoring:

Availability Monitoring: Ensuring the API is accessible and responding as expected, with checks to see if endpoints are live or returning the correct status codes (like 200 for success, or 404/500 for errors).

Performance Monitoring:

- **Latency:** Measuring the time, it takes for the API to process requests. High latency may indicate performance issues.
- **Throughput:** Monitoring the number of API requests processed within a given time to detect spikes or drops in traffic.
- **Error Rates:** Tracking error responses (e.g., 4xx or 5xx status codes) that could indicate problems like invalid requests, rate-limiting, or server-side issues.

Security Monitoring:

- **Rate Limiting & Throttling:** Monitoring unusual traffic patterns or high request volumes that could indicate abuse or attacks like denial of service (DoS).
- **Authentication and Authorization:** Ensuring that access tokens, API keys, and other security measures are functioning properly, and unauthorized access attempts are blocked.
- **Data Leaks or Breaches:** Detecting sensitive data exposure or other security vulnerabilities.
- **Functional Monitoring:** Periodically testing the functionality of API endpoints to ensure they return the expected results, often using predefined test cases or scripts.
- **Dependency Monitoring:** Keeping track of third-party services or systems that the API depends on, ensuring they remain available and performant.

- **Logging & Analytics:** Capturing and analyzing logs from API requests to identify trends, usage patterns, and anomalies, helping detect issues like slow response times or high error rates before they impact end-users.
- **Automation and Alerts:** Automatically triggering alerts or initiating corrective actions (such as scaling infrastructure or restarting services) when anomalies are detected.

Benefits of proactive monitoring:

Benefits of proactive API monitoring include:

- Reduced downtime by addressing issues before they escalate.
- Better user experience through consistent API performance and availability.
- Enhanced security by catching vulnerabilities or suspicious activities early.
- Optimized performance via trend analysis and scaling resources accordingly.

Reactive Monitoring:

Reactive monitoring is akin to diagnostic test and screenings performed when a health issue is observed. The diagnostic test and screenings are used for identifying the root cause of the disease in the body.

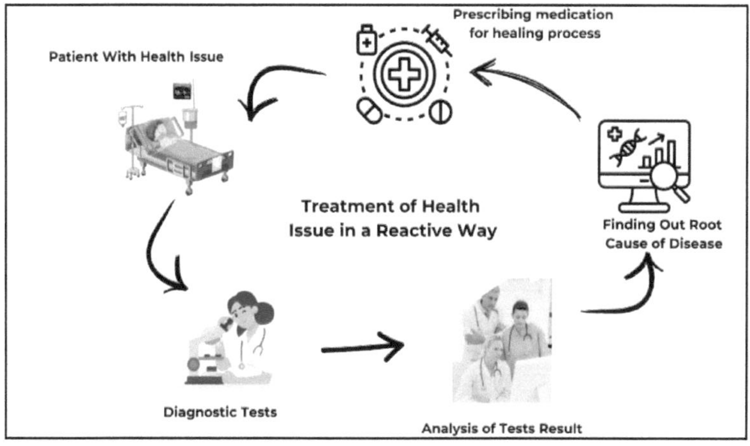

Figure 2.2 - Reactive Health Care

Reactive monitoring is a process of identifying and investigating incidents after they have occurred. This investigation is called root cause analysis (RCA). RCA is performed to understand what went wrong so that similar issue can be prevented in the future. This approach involves analyzing audit and debug logs, performance metrices to determine their causes and implement corrective action. Just like human health issue treatment process, API issue resolution also has a standard process which is followed to resolve the issue. Following diagram shows a typical way of API issue resoluton in a reactive way:

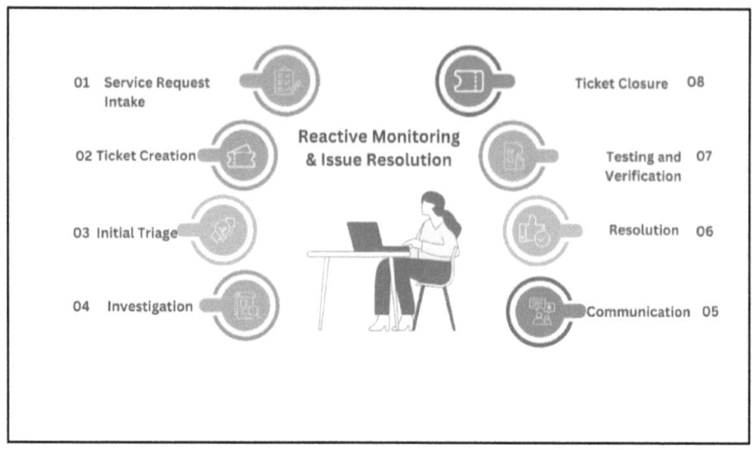

Figure 2.3 - API Issue Resolution Reactive Way

An incident occurs in production environment. SR/SRQ is created. It is assigned to a support team. Someone from the team picks it up and starts analysis of incident based on the input provided. If needed support engineer collaborate with the other teams and business team to understand the incident, if it is not a technical error. He provides the fix, testing/user acceptance testing is performed. New change is deployed to production. Incident is closed.

Key Characteristics:

- **Responsive:** Addresses issues after they are detected.
- **Incident-driven:** Triggered by alerts, user reports, or system failures.
- **Troubleshooting:** Involves root cause analysis and problem resolution.

Examples of reactive monitoring:

- **Incident reporting:** Collecting detailed reports of incidents when they occur. This includes business users, or automated systems documenting what happened.
- **Data Analysis:** Reviewing and analyzing the incident data to identify root cause of the issue.
- **Corrective Actions:** Developing and implementing measures to address the identified causes and prevent recurrence. This can include change in procedures, training, code modification, server restart etc.
- **Follow-Up:** Monitoring the effectiveness of the corrective action and making further adjustments if necessary. This step ensures that the measures taken are successful in preventing future incidents.
- Reactive monitoring is an important part of IT operation and support.

Benefits of reactive monitoring:

- It is cost effective as compared to proactive monitoring as it requires minimal resources.
- Provides insights into recurring problems for future prevention.
- Helps in quick incident resolution by utilizing

Reactive monitoring is essential for addressing unexpected or unpredictable issues. In MuleSoft APIs, monitoring refers to the process of tracking and analyzing various metrics and data points related to the performance, availability, and usage of APIs built on the MuleSoft Anypoint Platform. This monitoring helps ensure that APIs are operating as expected and meeting the needs of users and applications that rely on them. In next chapter, we will see, component and features provided by Anypoint platform for proactive and reactive monitoring.

3. MuleSoft Anypoint Monitoring Components

In the Anypoint Platform by MuleSoft, several monitoring features are available to help track the health, performance, and operations of your APIs, integrations, and applications. Using Anypoint Platform monitoring tool, support, development or administrator can get the visibility into the integration across your API/Application network. Intended team, can configure dashboard and alerts to reduce the mean time for identification of issues. They can also search the log data and co-relate the logs to identify the issues. Monitoring features vary, based on the Control plane instance. These features can be leveraged to monitor APIs in both reactive as well as proactive way. Here are the key monitoring components & features:

Proactive Monitoring Feature - Alerts

MuleSoft Anypoint Platform provides a feature for configuring various type of alerts. These alerts notifie whether MuleSoft APIs/Applications are behaving as expected or not. If APIs/Applications are not behaving as expected, alerts are raised, and email notification is triggered. Notification message explains the root cause of unexpected behavior. This may arise either due to underlying resource configuration or due to other configurations such as policy violation, response code violation etc. Alerts are categorized broadly into two categories:

1. **Basic Alerts:** It is created to trigger email notification when a specific metric threshold crosses the defined limit. Basic alerts are configured for APIs on API manager, or it is configured for Applications/APIs on Runtime

manager. We will talk about following basic operational alerts in more details going forward.

- API Manager Operational Alerts
- Runtime Manager Operational Alerts

2. **Advanced Alerts:** Advanced alerts within Anypoint Monitoring allow for more granular and customizable email notifications when metrics in custom dashboards exceed defined thresholds, offering more control over alerting than basic alerts.

Operational Alerts via API Manager:

Follow the steps to configure it manually:

- Login to https://anyppoint.mulesoft.com/login. Navigate to Business Group.

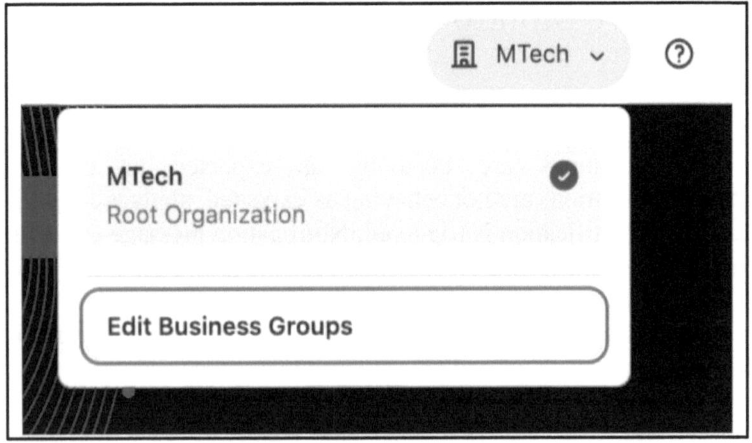

Figure 3.1 -Business Group

- Click on the API Manager

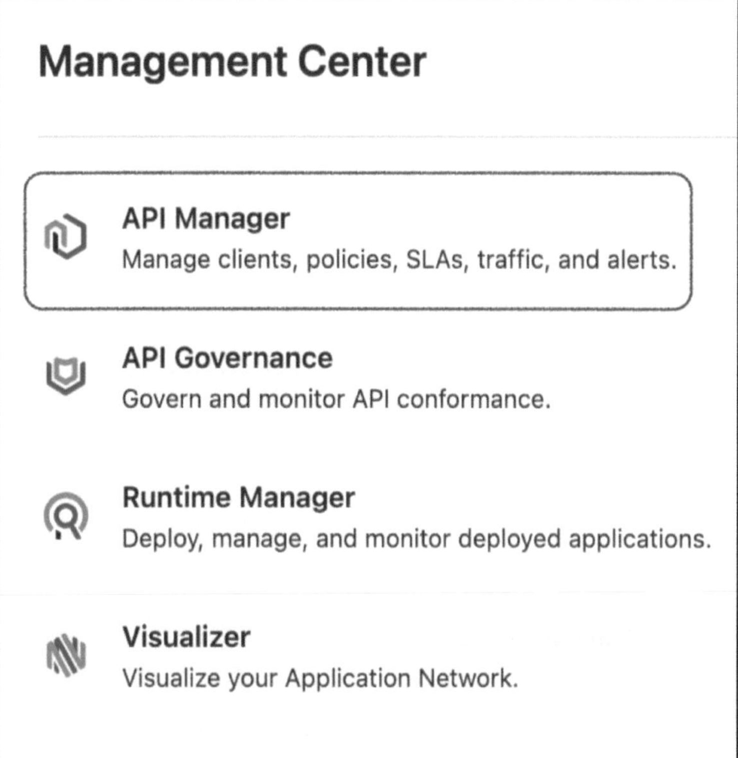

Figure 3.2 -API Manager

- Select environment and click on the specific API. Alert option will be available on left pane of the page.

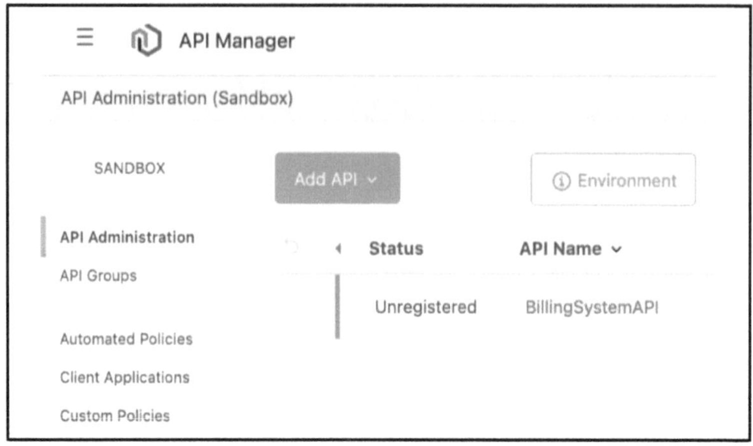

Figure 3.3 - Selected Envrionment

- Click on the Alert > Add alert
- Configure the alert options:
    - **Name**: Type an alert name, for example cpu-utilization-alert. If adding multiple alerts to the same environment, the alerts must have unique names
    - **Enabled**: The default option is **Enabled**.
    - You can delete an alert anytime, if not required.
    - **Severity**: Select a severity for the alert, for example, **Info, Warning or Critical**.
    - **Alert type**: Select the type of alert to create, (for example, Total **Request Count, Average Response Time etc.**) and provide appropriate alert configuration values.

- Alerts can be created on the following metrics in API manager:
    - Total Request Count
    - Average Response Time
    - Response Codes
    - Policy Violation
- Configure the condition for alert generation. Do you want to generate the alert, if it occurs once in a specific timeframe or 5 times in a specific timeframe. Configure the recipients of the alerts and save it. **You are all set to receive the alert,** if the alert condition, defined by you, is met. Support engineer, as soon as sees the alert, he/she can take proactive action and fix the issue before it gets converted into incident and impacts business.

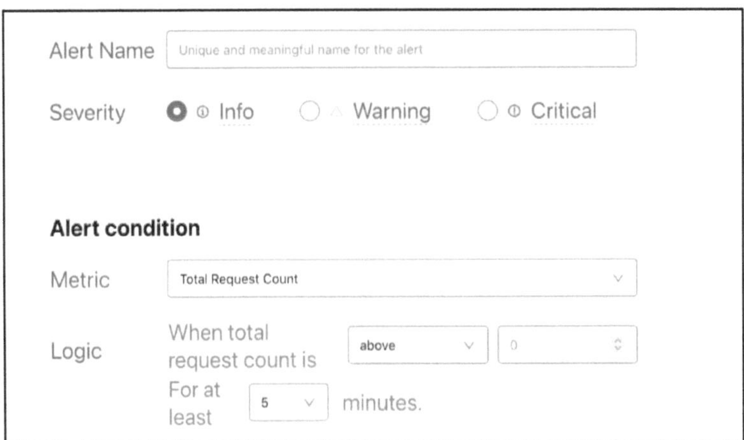

Figure 3.4 - Alert Condition

Operational Alerts via Anypoint Monitoring

- Go to Anypoint Monitoring > Alerts
- Create a new alert
- Click on basic alert
- Configure alert name (e.g. CPUUtilization-BillingSystemAPI)
- Select alert severity level (Info, Warning, Critical) from drop-down list
- Select resource type as Application, Server or API
- Select environment
- Select API name for which alert is to be created
- Select appropriate version of api
- Add alert condition
- Customize the notification header and body, if needed, or it can be left as default.
- Choose a notification channel (Email, Slack, PagerDuty, OpsGenie).
- Create alert.

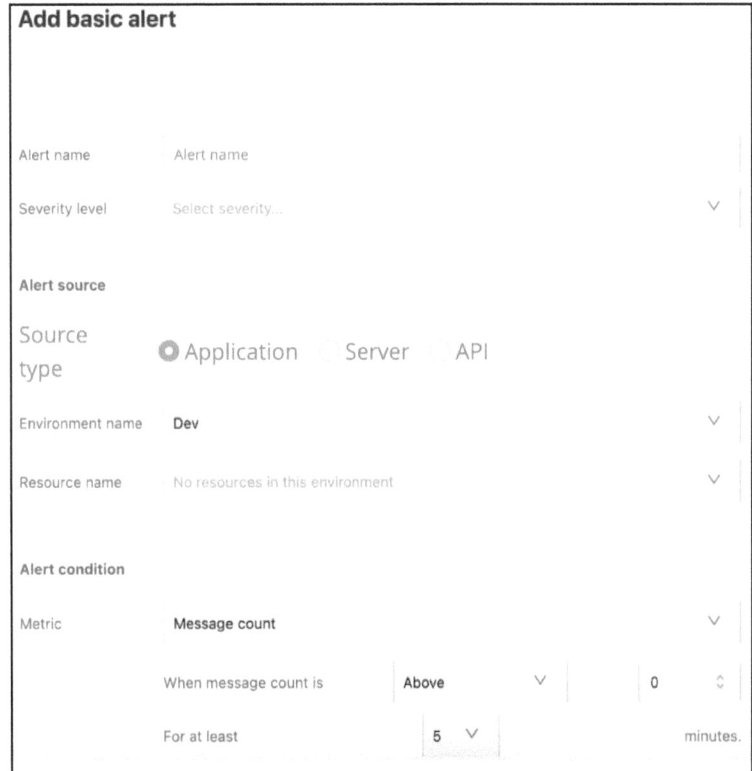

Figure 3.5 - Basic Alert

Operational Alerts via Runtime Manager

To monitor the health of applications, deployed on either CloudHub, Hybrid or RTF in a proactive manner, alerts can be created. Not only applications but servers, server groups and server clusters can also be monitored using alerts.

Alerts are triggered when a certain event occurs, and condition is met. Relevant team can be notified via email with the description of the events. We will see how to create alerts to get email notifications.

We will also see how to configure various type of conditions for different deployment models. To set up alert follow the steps

- Login to https://anypoint.mulesoft.com/login. Navigate to a particular business group
- Navigate to Management Cetner and select Runtime Manager
- Select the environment, in this example environment is SANDBOX.
- Click on alert from left pane

Figure 3.6 - Create Alert

- Click on "create your first alert". This option is available when there is no alert created.
- Name of the alert must be unique; hence you must be careful while providing a meaningful name. You can name it with the application name and condition to make it unique.

- For Example:
    - CPU-Utilization-BillingSystemAPI
    - CustomNotification-BillingSystemAPI

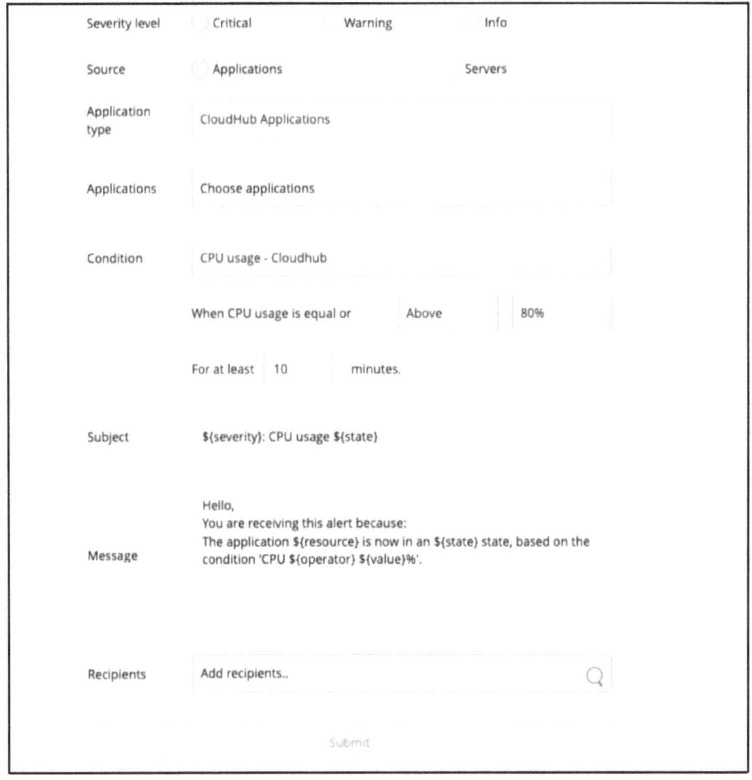

Figure 3.7 - Alert Config

As mentioned above these alerts can be configured for applications or servers. If you are creating alerts to monitor applications deployed in Anypoint CloudHub, Hybrid or RTF, you must select Applications otherwise Servers. Now there are three possible deployment models which can exist in any organizations. Select the one which appropriate for you. If your APIs are running in

CloudHub, select CloudHub otherwise whichever deployment model is being followed in your organization, you must select that. Application names drop down will show the APIs and Applications for which you want to configure alerts. Select the one for which you want to configure the alert. Following section will guide you on configuration details of different conditions for different deployment models.

Application Based Alerts for CloudHub APIs

Alerts for CPU Utilization:

This alert is configured to get notification when CPU utilization crosses the threshold configured. Suppose as depicted in the above screenshot, threshold is configured as 80% and condition is set to trigger alert when CPU Utilization exceeds 80% for 10 minutes. Whenever this condition is met an email notification is triggered to recipients. There can be more than one recipient configured.By default, subject of the email notification is ***${severity}: CPU usage ${state}***.

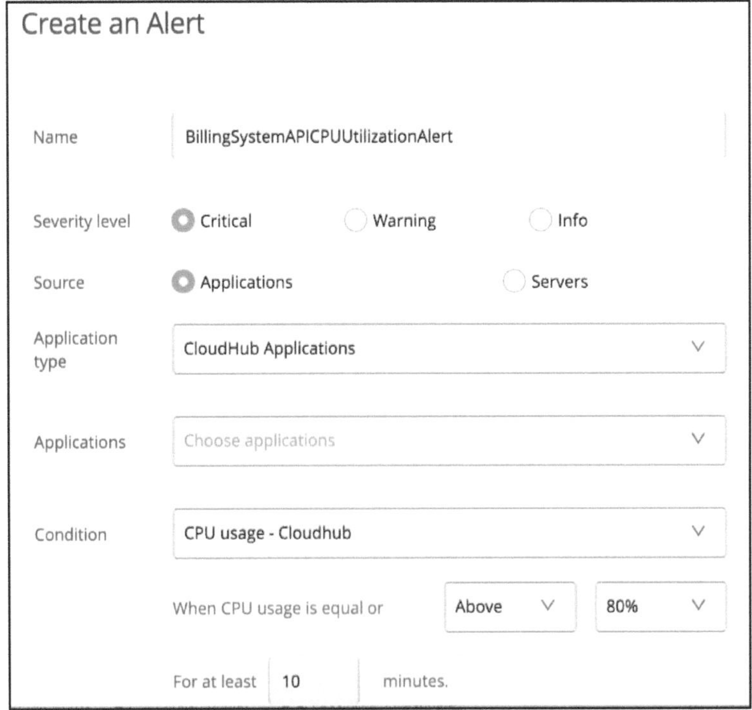

Figure 3.8 - CPU Utilization Alert

It can be modified to the subject of your preference. For example: notification for "BillingSystemAPI with ${severity}: CPU utilization ${state}" Or It is up to you, to configure the subject of the email notification. Similarly default email body is as follows:

> *Hello,*
>
> *You are receiving this alert because:*

The application ${resource} is now in an ${state} state, based on the condition 'CPU ${operator} ${value}%'.

However, this can be modified as per your requirement. You can utilize alert variables and define your own email template for alert notification. Other application alert condition is as follows:

Alerts for Worker Not Responding:

This alert is configured to get notification when a worker in CloudHub is not responding. Which means, when a request is sent to the worker, it does not get processed. This alert sends notification with name of the API/Application which is not responding. Below are the use cases.

- Detect unresponsive workers that could impact API availability.
- Identify server crashes, resource exhaustion, or network failures.
- Ensure high availability and auto-recovery of deployed applications.

Alerts for Deployment Failure:

This alert is setup to send notification for unsuccessful deployment of an API/Application in CloudHub deployment model. Below are the use cases.

- Detect failed deployments due to configuration errors, resource constraints, or platform issues.
- Ensure continuous deployment monitoring for API reliability.

- Identify and resolve infrastructure or permission-related problems.

Alerts for Deployment Success:

This alert is setup to send notification for successful deployment of an API/Application in CloudHub deployment model. Below are the use cases.

- Confirm successful deployments for tracking and auditing.
- Ensure deployment pipelines are functioning correctly.
- Notify teams when a new version of an API or application is live.

Exceeds Event Traffic Threshold

This alert is setup to send notification when number of business events exceeds the threshold defined. Below are the use cases.

- Detect unexpected spikes in API traffic that may impact performance.
- Identify potential DDoS attacks or misuse of API endpoints.
- Ensure scalability and load balancing to handle increased demand.

> This use case can be implemented in another way also. We can setup a Rate Limit Policy or Spike Control Policy in API Manager.
> Once the policy is setup, we can create a Policy Violation alertin API Manager for Rate Limit Policy or Spike Control Policy.

Application Based Alerts for On-Prem APIs

This option can be leveraged to use the MuleSoft Runtime Manager to configure alerts for your on-premises Mule Applications/APIs.

Alerts for Response Time:

This alert can be configured for sending email notification, if more than a specified number of errors observed in the APIs deployed in on-prem server. For example, alert gets triggered, if response time is equal or higher than time configured (millisecond). Below are the use cases.

- Detect slow API responses that may impact user experience.
- Identify backend performance issues, slow database queries, or high load.
- Ensure optimal response times for API consumers.

Alerts for Number of Mule Messages:

This alert is configured if the number of Mule Messages are exceeding a certain limit.
There are other ways available to generate similar alert. The same functionalities can be achieved in two step process. First configuring the Rate Limit policy on API manager. Second step is to configure policy violation alert for Rate Limit policy.
However, this configuration of alert in Runtime Manager is for on-prem server and it is triggered when API receives more than threshhold value defined in alert configuration. For example, configure condition to trigger an alert, if the number of messages received are greater than 1000 messages. Below are the use cases.

- Detect unexpected message surges that may impact performance.
- Identify potential system overloads or anomalies in processing.
- Ensure scalability and load balancing of MuleSoft applications.

Alerts for Application Undeployed:

This alert can be configured for sending email notification, if an application is undeployed. Below are the use cases.

- Detect accidental undeployment of application.

Alerts for Deployment Success/Failure:

Similar to CloudHub API/Application deplouyment Sucess/Failure Alert. Email notification is triggered in both the cases.

Application Alert for MuleSoft APIs/Applications Deployed on CloudHub 2.0 and RTF

In this deployment model, we get an option to create only two types of alert.

- Deployment Success
- Deployment Failure

Alert for Server Health Check:

Alerts can be setup for notifying the support engineers, if there is issue observed with server health. This can be configured for the stand-alone server, for servers in a group or for servers in cluster. Lets see these alerts and use cases in details.

Figure 3.9 - Runtime Agent Version Changed Alert

Runtime Manager Agent Version Changed Alert:

Runtime Manager agent is used as Mule runtime engine plug-in that enables communication with Mule runtime engine. You can use the agent to monitor and control Mule instances by calling the Runtime Manager agent APIs from external systems and having Mule publish its data to external systems. It can be utilized to get list of Application/APIs, status of Deployment/Undeployment/Start/Stop of Applications/APIs. This is also used to publish Mule metrics to external analystics system.

This alert is triggered when the Mule agent version changes. It helps detect unexpected upgrades, downgrades, or unauthorized modifications to the runtime environment. Below are the use cases.

- Monitor planned vs. unplanned agent version updates.
- Ensure correct agent version is running.

Runtime Version Changed Alert

This alert is triggered when the Mule runtime version of an application changes. It helps detect unexpected upgrades, downgrades, or unauthorized modifications to the runtime environment. Below are the use cases.

- Monitor planned vs. unplanned runtime updates.
- Ensure applications run on the correct Mule version.
- Prevent compatibility issues due to unexpected version changes.

Server CPU Usage Alert

This alert is triggered when the CPU usage of a MuleSoft server exceeds a defined threshold, indicating potential performance issues or resource exhaustion. Below are the use cases.

- Detect high CPU utilization that may impact application performance.
- Identify resource bottlenecks and optimize server capacity.
- Prevent downtime due to excessive processing load.

Server Load Alert

This alert is triggered when the server load handling MuleSoft APIs exceeds a defined threshold, indicating high traffic, resource strain, or potential performance degradation. Below are the use cases.

- Monitor high request loads on MuleSoft APIs.
- Identify scalability issues and prevent slowdowns.
- Ensure API availability and performance under heavy traffic.

Server Memory Usage Alert

This alert is triggered when the server memory usage for a MuleSoft API exceeds a defined threshold, indicating potential memory leaks, inefficient resource usage, or high workload. Below are the use cases.

- Detect high memory consumption affecting API performance.
- Prevent OutOfMemory (OOM) errors and application crashes.
- Optimize memory allocation for better efficiency.

Server Thread Count Alert

This alert is triggered when the server thread count for a MuleSoft API exceeds a defined threshold, indicating potential thread exhaustion, concurrency issues, or high load. Below are the use cases.

- Detect excessive thread usage that may lead to performance degradation.
- Prevent thread pool exhaustion, which can cause API slowdowns or failures.

- Identify inefficient threading configurations in MuleSoft applications.

Server Connected Alert

This alert is triggered when a MuleSoft server instance connects or reconnects after being offline. It helps track server availability and unexpected restarts. Below are the use cases.

- Monitor server uptime and reconnections.
- Detect unexpected restarts or failover events.
- Ensure high availability of MuleSoft APIs.

Server Deleted Alert

This alert is triggered when a MuleSoft server instance is deleted from the environment, either manually or due to an automated process. It helps track unexpected server removals that may impact API availability. Below are the use cases.

- Detect unauthorized or accidental server deletions.
- Ensure infrastructure integrity and compliance.
- Prevent unexpected downtime due to server removal.

Server Disconnected Alert

This alert is triggered when a MuleSoft server instance disconnects, indicating potential network issues, server crashes, or unexpected shutdowns. Below are the use cases.

- Detect server failures or downtime.
- Identify network or infrastructure issues.

- Ensure high availability of MuleSoft APIs.

Server Group Alert

This alert is triggered when a server group status changes, such as when a server joins, leaves, or becomes unavailable within a MuleSoft server group. It helps monitor cluster health and availability. Below are the use cases.

- *Detect server failures or unexpected removals from the group.*
- *Ensure high availability for APIs running on clustered environments.*
- *Monitor scalability events, such as new servers being added or removed.*

Server Group Connected Alert

This alert is triggered when a server group successfully connects in MuleSoft server group, indicating that all required servers in the group are online and available. Below are the use cases.

- Confirm successful startup of a clustered MuleSoft environment.
- Ensure API services are fully operational.
- Detect when a previously unavailable server group reconnects.

Server Group Deleted Alert

This alert is triggered when a server group is deleted in MuleSoft, indicating a manual removal or an automated infrastructure change. Monitoring this ensures that no critical environments are accidentally removed. Below are the use cases.

- Detect unauthorized or accidental deletion of a server group.
- Prevent unexpected service disruptions due to missing server groups.
- Maintain infrastructure integrity and compliance.

Server Group Disconnected Alert

This alert is triggered when a server group becomes disconnected in MuleSoft server group, indicating that all or a majority of the servers in the group have lost connectivity. This could be due to network failures, infrastructure issues, or server crashes. Below are the use cases.

- Detect server group failures or downtime affecting API availability.
- Identify network or infrastructure issues causing disconnections.
- Ensure high availability and reliability of MuleSoft applications.

Server Group Node Average Load Alert

This alert is triggered when the average load across nodes in a MuleSoft server group exceeds a defined threshold. It helps monitor server performance and prevent potential resource exhaustion. Below are the use cases.

- Detect high workload on server group nodes.
- Identify performance bottlenecks affecting API response times.
- Ensure optimal load balancing across nodes.

Server Group Node Memory Usage Alert

This alert is triggered when the memory usage of one or more nodes in a MuleSoft server group exceeds a defined threshold. It helps monitor resource consumption and prevent performance degradation. Below are the use cases.

- Detect high memory usage that may cause slowdowns or crashes.
- Identify memory leaks or inefficient resource allocation.
- Ensure optimal performance of APIs running on the server group.

Server Group Node Thread Count Alert

This alert is triggered when the thread count of one or more nodes in a MuleSoft server group exceeds a defined threshold. It helps monitor thread usage and prevent performance issues caused by excessive threading. Below are the use cases.

- Detect high thread utilization that may lead to slowdowns or failures.
- Identify thread pool exhaustion, which can impact API performance.
- Ensure efficient thread management in MuleSoft applications.

Server Group Node Connected Alert

This alert is triggered when a node successfully connects to a MuleSoft server group, indicating that the node is online and available for processing requests. Below are the use cases.

- Confirm new node additions to the server group.

- Detect previously disconnected nodes reconnecting.
- Ensure high availability and proper scaling of MuleSoft applications.

Server Group Node Disconnected Alert

This alert is triggered when a node disconnects from a MuleSoft server group, indicating potential network issues, server crashes, or infrastructure failures.

- Detect node failures or unexpected disconnections.
- Identify network or infrastructure issues affecting API availability.
- Ensure high availability of MuleSoft applications by monitoring node health.

Server Group Server Added Alert

This alert is triggered when a new server is added to a MuleSoft server group, indicating a scaling event or infrastructure change. Below are the use cases

- Monitor auto-scaling events or manual server additions.
- Ensure proper load distribution within the server group.
- Track infrastructure changes for compliance and security.

Server Group Server Removed Alert

This alert is triggered when a server is removed from a MuleSoft server group, indicating a potential scaling event, manual removal, or unexpected infrastructure change. Below are the use cases

- Detect unauthorized or accidental server removal.

- Ensure high availability by monitoring server group health.
- Track infrastructure changes for security and compliance.

Anypoint Insights

It is available for Titanium Tier customers. This is a feature in MuleSoft's Anypoint Platform designed to provide visibility into API performance, usage, and analytics. It helped organizations monitor API traffic, track response times, identify bottlenecks, and analyze user behavior. It will be useful, if a support engineer is monitoring Anypoint insights frequently or at a defined time interval. Otherwise this feature become reactive monitoring feature.

Figure 3.10 - Anypoint Insights

There are various useful and important metrics available. These metrics can be utilized to monitor the API/Application health and performance.

Anypoint Custom Dashboard

It is a feature within Anypoint Monitoring that allows users to create personalized dashboards to monitor API and Application performance. It provides flexibility in visualizing key metrics, enabling teams to track specific data points relevant to their Infrastructure, APIs, and Integrations. With Custom Dashboards, users can:

- Select and display specific metrics, such as response times, error rates, CPU/memory usage, and traffic trends.
- Create customized visualizations using charts, graphs, and tables for real-time insights.
- Monitor APIs, Mule applications, and hybrid deployments in one unified view.
- Set up alerts and thresholds for proactive monitoring and issue resolution.

This feature helps organizations tailor monitoring to their specific needs, ensuring efficient performance tracking and faster troubleshooting.

Custom Dashboard Setup

You can configure custom dashboard to display API/Application metrics in graphical form, as a single stats, in a tabular form, text form or mixed of all.
We will take one example presenting count of messages received for a perticualr resource in the Billing System API and response time to process the request. Let's say, from our initial example of api-led

integration solution, we want to present number of request received for GET /unbilledAmount for BillingSystemAPI and Response Time.You need to understand, there are some metrics data available from API Manager and Some of the data is available from Runtime Manager.

- Follow the steps to configure custom dashboard:
    - Navigate to Anypoint monitoring -> Custom Dashboards -> New Dashboard

For above mentioned scenario, you can select either graph or table as per your prefernce.

Configure the following details for number of request received:

- Select "Advanced Mode"
- Select Panel Type = "API Panel" and query field From = "api_summary_metric"
- Use "api_id" and "api_version_id" to point to the API you want to monitor
- Select "request_size.count" for the field, as we are looking for total number of messages here
- Add the tags "count" and "path" for the Group by element
- Finally, for a better visual reading on the graph, use the alias "$tag_count $tag_path"

Simlarly for response time metrics configure the following details:

- Select "Advanced Mode"
- Select Panel Type = "API Panel" and query field From = "api_summary_metric"

- Use "api_id" and "api_version_id" to point to the API you want to monitor, then add "/unbilledAmount" on the endpoints you want to monitor.
- Select "response_time.avg" for the field, as we are looking for avg response time here
- Add the tags "methods" and "path" for the Group by element
- Finally, for a better visual reading on the graph, use the alias "$tag_method $tag_path"

Custom dashbaord is useful when a support engineer wants to monitor certain APIs/Applications for a specific metric data. He/she can utilize this dashboard to proactivly monitor the APIs/Applications in a defined time interval.

Reactive Monitoring feature

Anypoint Monitoring is MuleSoft's built-in observability tool that helps track API performance, health, and application logs. It is available for CloudHub, Hybrid, and RTF MuleSoft deployments.We have talked on earlier section about proactive feature of monitoring which is alert and Insights. In this section we will see reactive monitoring features as depicted in the below diagram:

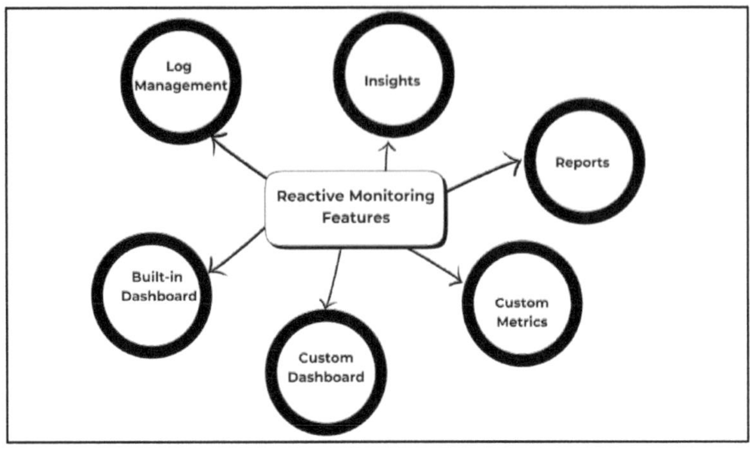

Figure 3.11 - Reactive Monitoring Features

Log Management

This feature is available for Titanium Subscription. Anypoint Monitoring aggregates log files of all the APIs. These log files can be utlized by support engineer, developer to search, filter and analyse logs. We will see the features available in Log Management.

Log Search

This feature comes with titanium tiers.

If you are using CloudHub environment to deployment your APIs. You can check the log in the following ways:

- Navigate to Runtime manager.
- Click on the API for which you want to see the logs. On the left side, you see the options for Logs

Figure 3.12 - Billing System API

- Click on the logs and log will be displayed

Figure 3.13 - Logs

- You can narrow down the time range for the log

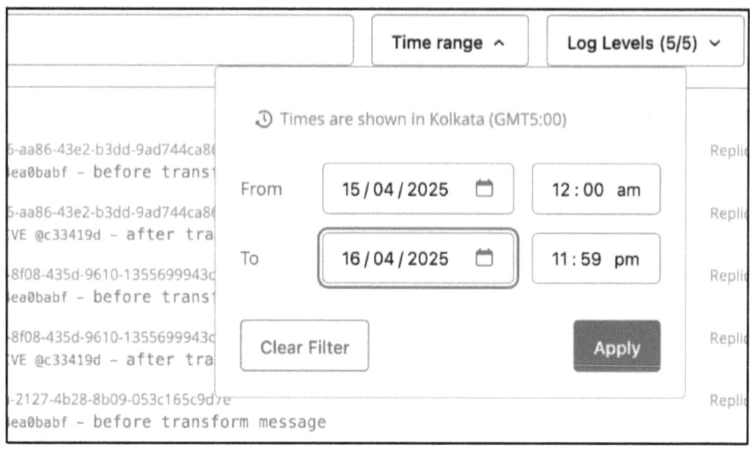

Figure 3.14 - Filter Based on Time Range

- You can use search bar to find out specific log. For example searching the customer id etc. In this example "before transform message" string is searched and related log is displayed.

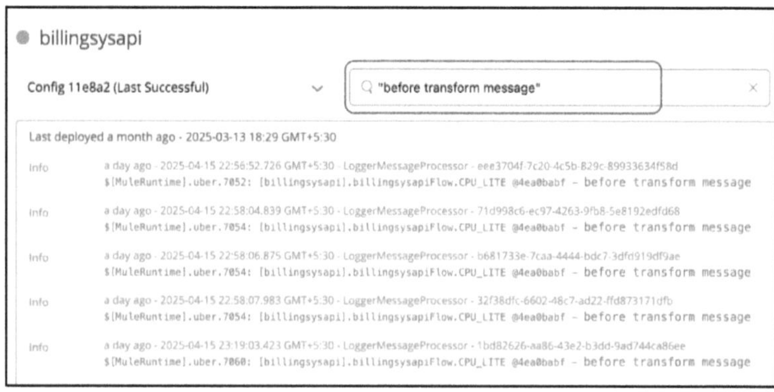

Figure 3.15 - Filtered Log

If you are using Titanium tier, you will have more rich functionality available for log management. You get Log Search, Log Points and Raw Data feature. You can use the advanced filter to narrow down your search as follows:

- Anypoint Monitoring > Log Management > Log Search > Add filter
- You can filter the log based on following criteria
    - application
    - class
    - environment
    - environment type
    - log level
    - logger
    - message
    - thread
    - timestamp
    - worker
- Select the operator from the drop-down list
- If applicable enter a value
- Click save

You will get logs as per your filter criteria.

Filter criteria can also be written as Query DSL. For example:

{"query": {“match": {"log-level": "query": "INFO",

"type": "phrase”}}}}

Note:

You get an option to see the log either in the format of JSON or Table. After finding a log for a particular issue, you might want to know what other log reports proceded or followed it.

Many a times, we get into a situation where verbose logging is required for various connectors. This helps in trouble shooting the issues. This process is called enabling the wire log or enabling DEBUG log

Enable Verbose (debug) Logging

Verbose logging can be enabled for different modules. This can be performed as follows:

- Navigate to Runtime manager
- Click on the api for which log has to be enabled
- Go to monitoring tab
- Select DEBUG from drop down and add package name. In this example we have demonstrated it for HTTP.

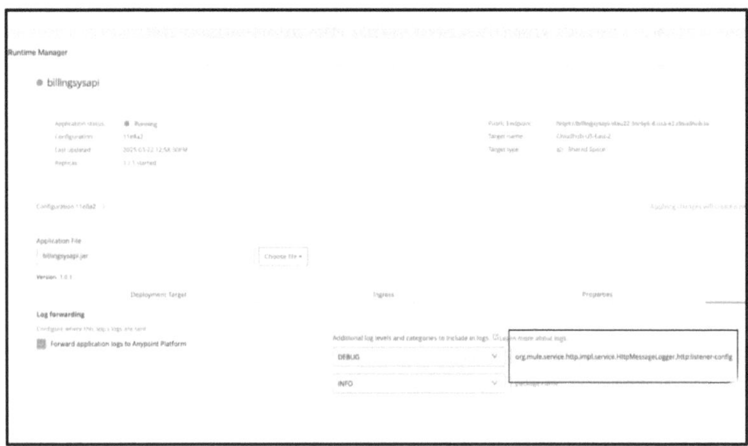

Figure 3.16 - Debug Package Name Configuration

- Click Apply Changes

These steps will enable verbose log and connector/module level verbose log is enabled. This can be used for debugging the issues. Refer to the list below to find out package name for enabling DEBUG log:

Amazon DynamoDB Connector	org.mule.extension.dynamodb org.mule.service.http.impl.service.HttpMessageLogger **Driver:** com.amazonaws com.amazonaws.services
Amazon RDS Connector	org.mule.extension.rds org.mule.service.http.impl.service.HttpMessageLogger org.apache.http **Driver:** com.amazonaws com.amazonaws.services
Amazon S3 Connector	org.mule.extension.s3 org.mule.service.http.impl.service.HttpMessageLogger **Driver:** com.amazonaws com.amazonaws.services
Amazon SNS Connector	org.mule.extension.sns org.mule.service.http.impl.service.HttpMessageLogger **Driver:** com.amazonaws com.amazonaws.services

Amazon SQS Connector	org.mule.extension.sqs org.mule.service.http.impl.service.HttpMessageLogger **Driver:** org.apache.http
AS2 Connector	com.mulesoft.connector.as2 org.mule.service.http.impl.service.HttpMessageLogger
HTTP Connector	org.mule.service.http.impl.service.HttpMessageLogger
JMS Connector	org.mule.extensions.jms org.mule.jms

If the DEBUG package name is not listed in the above table, please proceed to do the following:

- Find the Connector/Module jar file in the project in Anypoint Studio under package explorer on the left side. The name of the jar file follows the patterns below:
    - "mule-<module name>-module-<version>-mule-plugin.jar" for Mule 4 Module
    - "mule-<connector name>-connector-<version>-mule-plugin.jar" for Mule 4 Connector

- If the jar file is not in the project yet, add the dependency to the project in Anypoint Studio and you will see the relevant jar files are downloaded to the project.

- Expand the jar file to view the Java package names. Examples:
- The below screenshot shows the mule-salesforce-connector-11.0.0-mule-plugin.jar file for the HTTP Connector and its package name "org.mule.extension.salesforce" that can be used to enable DEBUG logs.

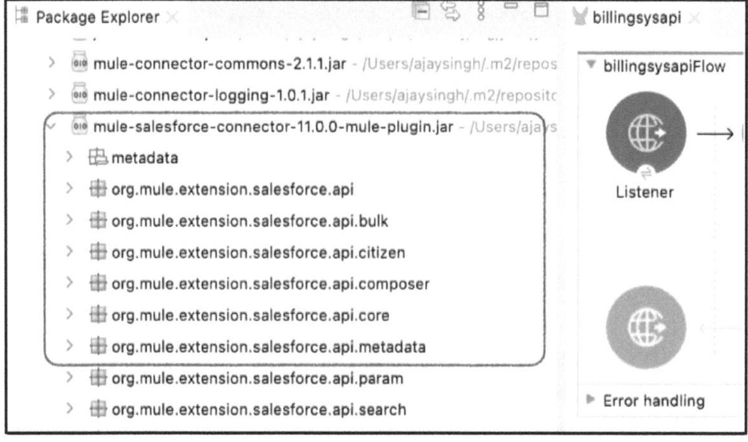

Figure 3.17 - Salesforce Connector Plugin Package

- From the below screenshot, you can see the list of modules for JMS connector v1.10.0 by double clicking on the connector name in package explorer. You will have to open the library and inspect its JAR files until finding one with the name of the Module/Connector. Inside that JAR, you can find all Mule related packages. In this case, for the JMS Module, you will find a mule-jms-connector JAR as on the image below:

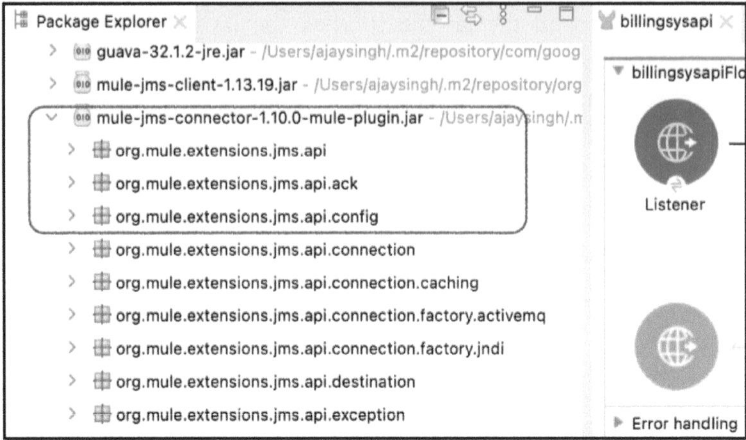

Figure 3.18 - JMS Connector Plugin Package

Raw Data

This feature is also available for Titanium Tier. You can use Anypoint Monitoring to download archived log data (raw data) collected for Mule APIs/Applications that are running in hybrid, CloudHub, or Runtime Fabric deployments. To download raw data:

- Select the **Environment** and **Resource.**

  Resource is a Mule API/Application that runs in CloudHub, hybrid, Runtime Fabric deployments.

- Provide the date for the data you want to download, for example: 03/31/2025.
- Locate and download log data that you want to examine.
- If data is not available for a particular date, it might be that the Application/API was not running that day, your company did not have a subscription to the logging or archiving service, or the Applicaiton/API did not exist at that time. Below are the use cases.

- To get the full payload in case the payload size is big and getting truncated on Log Search page. You can download raw data and open it in editor to see the complete payload.
- You can download and store it for compliance requirement

Built-in Dashboard

This is another component used for reactive monitoring. To explore the default observability follow the steps mentioned.

- Navigate to Monitoring in Anypoint Platform.
- Click on the Built-in dashboards

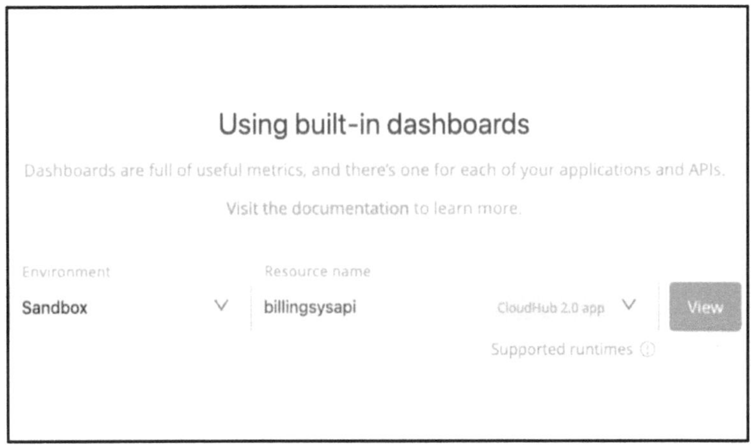

Figure 3.19 - Built-in Dasboard

- Select the environment and API and click view. You will see different metrices available for API. If there is no traffic you will see these metrices as blank.

Please note, image presented is from trial account which does not have all the dashboard listed. If you are Titanium customer, there will be few more dashboard apart from Overview, Inound, Outbound, Performance, Failure, JVM and Infrastructure. Those extra ones are Flows, Connectors, Custom Metrics and Application Network.

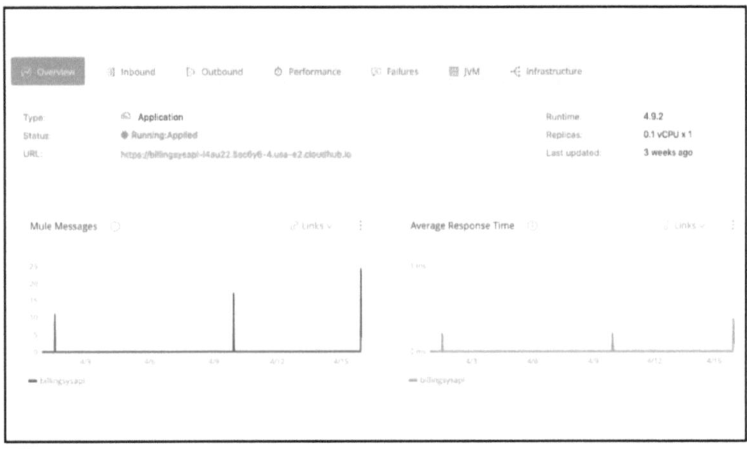

Figure 3.20 - Dashboard Metrics

- If traffic is available, metrics is visible - No. of MuleMessages, Average Response Time, Error
- CPU Utilization, Memory Utilization, Thread Utilization

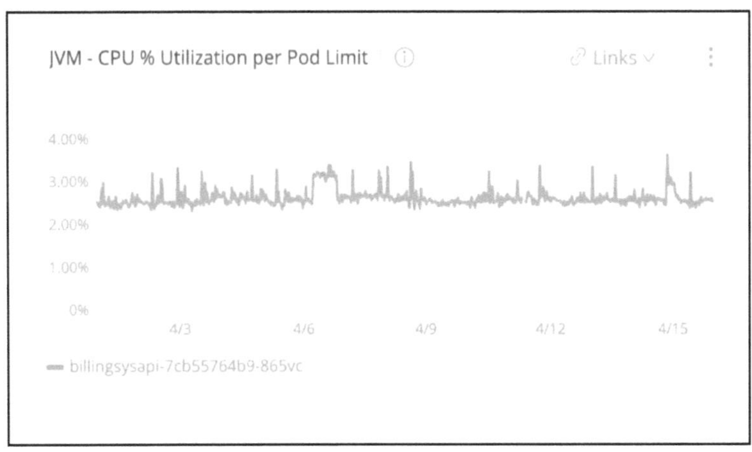

Figure 3.21 - Metrics View

Dashboard charts are very much self explainatory and it is highly useful for anlysing performance issues.

Overview Dashboard presents following metrics:

- *Average Response Time*
- *Errors*
- *Inbound - Total Requests by Response Type*
- *Inbound - Average Response Time*
- *Outbound - Total Requests by Response Type*
- *Outbound - Average Response Time*
- *JVM - CPU % Utilization*
- *JVM - Heap Used*
- *JVM - Thread Count*

Inbound Dashboard presents following metrics:

- *Inbound - Total Requests by Response Type*

- *Inbound - Average Response Time*
- *Inbound - Response Time by HTTP Endpoint*
- *Inbound - Total Requests by Endpoint*
- *Inbound - Response Time graphs (99, 90, 75, and 50 percentiles)*
- *Inbound - Total Failed Requests*

Outbound Dashboard presents following metrics:

- *Outbound - Total Requests by Response Type*
- *Outbound - Average Response Time*
- *Outbound - Average Response Time by HTTP Endpoint*
- *Outbound - Total Requests by HTTP Endpoint*
- *Outbound - Response Time graphs (99, 90, 75, and 50 percentiles)*
- *Outbound - Total Failed Requests*

Flows Dashboard presents following metrics:

- *Inbound - Response Time by Flow*
- *Outbound - Response Time by Flow*
- *Inbound - Requests by Flow*
- *Outbound - Requests by Flow*
- *Failures by Flow*
- *Inbound - Slow Requests by Flow*
- *Outbound - Slow Requests by Flow*
- *Inbound - Response Time by Flow*
- *Outbound - Response Time by Flow*
- *Inbound - Requests by Flow*
- *Outbound - Requests by Flow*
- *Failures by Flow*
- *Inbound - Slow Requests by Flow*
- *Outbound - Slow Requests by Flow*

Connector specific metrics are required if we want to debug and anlyze the behaviour of connector.

Connector Dashboard presents following metrics:

- *Connector Message Volume*
- *Response Time by Connector*
- *Salesforce Requests*
- *Salesforce Response Time*
- *Database Requests*
- *Database Response Time*
- *HTTP Requests*
- *HTTP Response Time*
- *HTTP Failures*
- *Web Services Requests*
- *Web Services Response Time*
- *Web Services Failures*
- *FTP Requests*
- *FTP Response Time*
- *FTP Failures*
- *SFTP Requests*
- *SFTP Response Time*
- *SFTP Failures*
- *SMTP Requests*
- *SMTP Response Time*
- *SMTP Failures*
- *Object Store Requests*
- *Object Store Response Time*
- *Object Store Failures*
- *Anypoint MQ Operations - Inbound*
- *Anypoint MQ Response Time - Inbound*
- *Anypoint MQ Failures - Inbound*
- *Anypoint MQ Operations - Outbound*
- *Anypoint MQ Response Time - Outbound*
- *Anypoint MQ Failures - Outbound*
- *Other Connector Requests*

- *Other Connector Response Time*
- *Other Connector Failures*

Performance Dashboard presents following metrics

- *Mule Messages*
- *Average Response Time*
- *Inbound-Average Response Time*
- *Inbound-Average Response Time by HTTP Endpoint*
- *Inbound-Min Response Time by HTTP Endpoint*
- *Inbound-Max Response Time by HTTP Endpoint*
- *Inbound-Response Time - 99 Percentile*
- *Inbound-Response Time - 90 Percentile*
- *Inbound-Response Time - 75 Percentile*
- *Inbound-Response Time - 50 Percentile*
- *Outbound-Average Response Time*
- *Outbound-Average Response Time by Endpoint*
- *Outbound-Min Response Time by Endpoint*
- *Outbound-Max Response Time by Endpoint*
- *Outbound-Response Time - 99 Percentile*
- *Outbound-Response Time - 90 Percentile*
- *Outbound-Response Time - 75 Percentile*
- *Outbound-Response Time - 50 Percentile*

Errors Dashboard presents following metrics:

- *Inbound- Failure Total Request Count*
- *Outbound-Failure Total Request Count*
- *Inbound- Total Requests by Response Type*
- *Outbound- Total Requests by Response Type*
- *Inbound- Failure Response Time by Endpoint*
- *Inbound- Failure Total Request Count by Endpoint*
- *Outbound- Failure Response Time by Endpoint*

- *Outbound- Failure Total Request Count by Endpoint*

JVM Dashboard Presents following metrics

- *Old Gen GC Count*
- *Old Gen GC Time*
- *Young Gen GC Count*
- *Young Gen GC Time*
- *Classes Loaded*
- *Classes Loaded Total*
- *Classes Unloaded*
- *Heap Committed*
- *Heap Used*
- *Thread Count*
- *JVM Uptime*
- *Eden Space graphs (Used, Max, Init, and Committed)*
- *Survivor Space graphs (Used, Max, Init, and Committed)*
- *Metaspace graphs (Used, Max, Init, Committed)*
- *Code Cache graphs (Used, Max, Init, Committed)*
- *Compressed Class Space graphs (Used, Max, Init, Committed)*
- *Old Gen Mem graphs (Used, Max, Init, Committed)*
- *Committed Virtual Memory*

Infrastructure Dashboard Metrics are as follows:

- *JVM - CPU % Utilization*
- *JVM - Heap Used*
- *Total System Processors*
- *System Memory*
- *JVM Thread Count*
- *System CPU % Utilization*
- *JVM CPU Time*

- *Operating System Swap Space*
- *These metrics can be exported in CSV file.*

These metrics data can be exported to a CSV file.

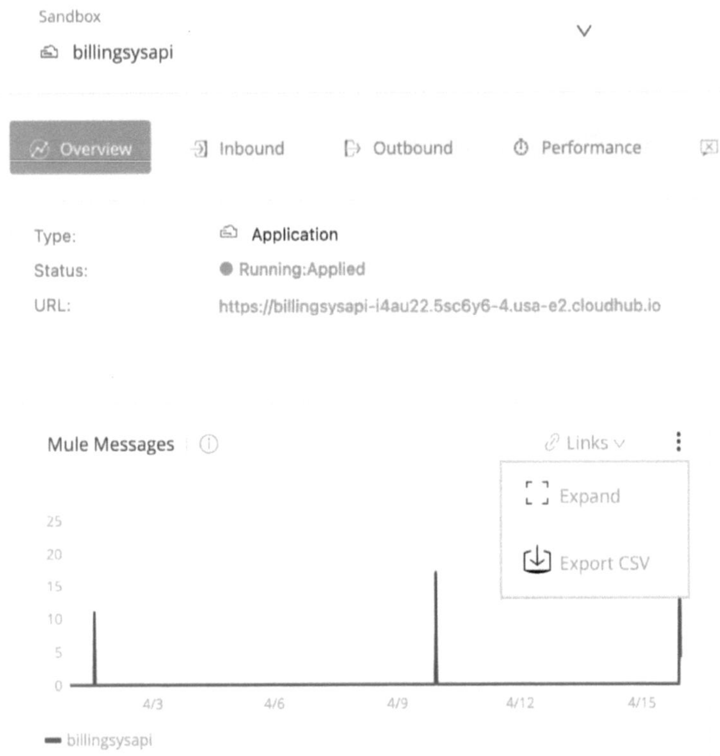

Figure 3.22 - Export CSV

Exported CSV file will look like:

AnypointMonitoringExport

sep=		
Series	Time	Value
billingsysapi-7cb55764b9-865vc	2025-03-23T18:51:00+05:30	null
billingsysapi-7cb55764b9-865vc	2025-03-23T18:52:00+05:30	47
billingsysapi-7cb55764b9-865vc	2025-03-23T18:53:00+05:30	48
billingsysapi-7cb55764b9-865vc	2025-03-23T18:54:00+05:30	47
billingsysapi-7cb55764b9-865vc	2025-03-23T18:55:00+05:30	50
billingsysapi-7cb55764b9-865vc	2025-03-23T18:56:00+05:30	47
billingsysapi-7cb55764b9-865vc	2025-03-23T18:57:00+05:30	47
billingsysapi-7cb55764b9-865vc	2025-03-23T18:58:00+05:30	48
billingsysapi-7cb55764b9-865vc	2025-03-23T18:59:00+05:30	47
billingsysapi-7cb55764b9-865vc	2025-03-23T19:00:00+05:30	47
billingsysapi-7cb55764b9-865vc	2025-03-23T19:01:00+05:30	47
billingsysapi-7cb55764b9-865vc	2025-03-23T19:02:00+05:30	47
billingsysapi-7cb55764b9-865vc	2025-03-23T19:03:00+05:30	48
billingsysapi-7cb55764b9-865vc	2025-03-23T19:04:00+05:30	47
billingsysapi-7cb55764b9-865vc	2025-03-23T19:05:00+05:30	null
billingsysapi-7cb55764b9-865vc	2025-03-23T19:06:00+05:30	null

Figure 3.23 - Exported CSV File

As these metrics are available for a specific time duration only, these downlaoded csv can be stored for longer duaration for audit purpose. Exporting Anypoint Dashboard Metrics to a CSV file can be useful in several scenarios, including analysis, reporting, compliance, and troubleshooting.

Custom Metrics

It is available for Advanced and Titanium Tier customer. Custom metrics presents operation or functional data. It is not available by default. You need to define the operational and funtional data which you want to send to Anypoint Monitoring and analyse it in the in-built dashboard.

To achieve this, you must use customer metrics connector in your API or Application code and map your operational or functional data.

- Add custom metrics connector from exachange

- Add custom metrics connector to your flow.Configure the Send Custom Metrics.

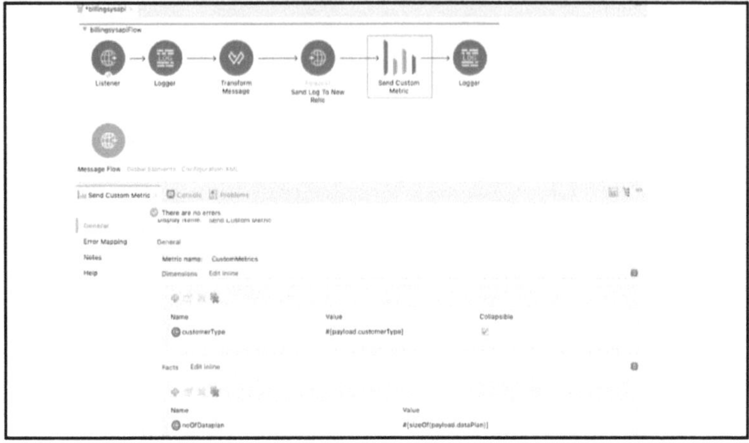

Figure 3.24 - Custom Metrics Connector

- Once you deploy your API/Application, navigate to Custom Metrics under inbuilt-dashboard. You will see a dashboard presenting custom metrics.
- In our example, you will can get a metrics of mobile customer type and number of data plans subscribed to.

Best Practices for Using Custom Metrics Connector

MuleSoft has suggested best practices while using custom metrics connector.

- Do not use restricted keyword while defining dimension and facts in API/Application code. Refer to https://docs.mulesoft.com for list of restricted keywords.

- Use low cardinality dimension which means, choose a field from payload which has low cardinality in terms of value. For example you must use country_code instead of location_code.

Application Network (Visualizer)

This dashboard represents visualization of API/Applicaiton network which means if your selected API has received request under last 7 days, This dashboard will show directly connected API/Application network. This migh be helpful in idenfying dependencies.

Figure 3.25 - Application Network

4. External Monitoring Tools

"Give me six hours to chop down a tree and I will spend the first four sharpening the axe." — Abraham Lincoln

External monitoring tools for MuleSoft API observability are essential for ensuring the performance, availability, and reliability. These tools provide visibility into the health of your MuleSoft runtime, Integrations, and Infrastructure. By continuously tracking key performance indicators, they help detect anomalies, identify potential bottlenecks, and mitigate risks before they impact business operations. With both proactive and reactive monitoring capabilities, these tools allow teams to respond swiftly to performance issues and system failures. Proactive monitoring helps prevent disruptions by identifying trends and addressing concerns in advance, while reactive monitoring ensures quick troubleshooting and resolution when unexpected issues arise. This comprehensive approach enhances operational efficiency and ensures a seamless experience for end users.

By default, when Mule APIs are deployed in the CloudHub, all logs are stored and managed directly in the CloudHub environment. This leads the API/Application Support Team to analyze the logs directly from the CloudHub environment. However, there is a limitation in terms of log retention for CloudHub deployment model. CloudHub stores logs up to 30 days/100 MB which reaches first. As per the audit and security governance compliance, the support team might need to analyze logs beyond the period. This leads to the loss of important log data after this threshold limit. For Application/API deployed in Runtime Fabric, if you want to monitor it in Anypoint Monitoring, you need to forward the logs of Application/API deployed in RTF to Anypoint Monitoring. In order to do that, you need to check your subscriptiontype and feature availability. It is quite straight forward configuration under Runtime Manager. There might be another need to co-locating logs of MuleSoft APIs/Application and Source/Target applicaiton at one place.

MuleSoft Anypoint Platform does not support the out-of-the-box way of storing log files to external log management. Below are some popular external monitoring tools that can be used:

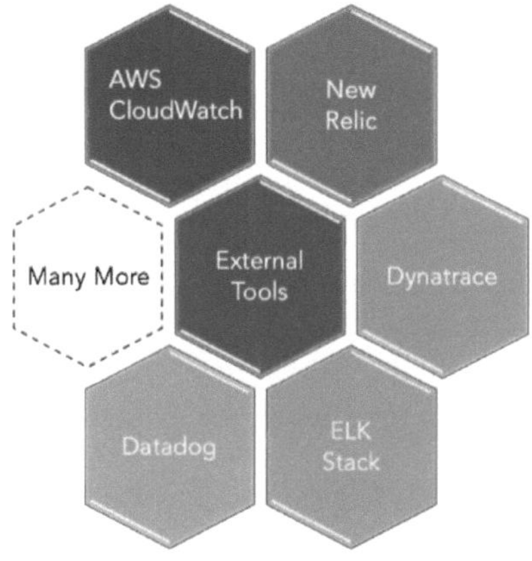

Figure 4.1 - External Monitoring Tools

Dynatrace Monitoring

Dynatrace is an advanced AI-powered observability platform designed to deliver comprehensive, end-to-end monitoring for various applications. It enables organizations to gain deep insights into their systems, ensuring optimal performance, security, and reliability. With its intelligent automation and real-time analytics,

Dynatrace helps teams proactively identify and resolve issues before they impact business operations.

When it comes to MuleSoft APIs and integrations, Dynatrace provides specialized monitoring capabilities that track API performance, detect anomalies, and optimize workflows. By offering detailed visibility into API transactions and dependencies, it enhances troubleshooting efficiency and ensures seamless connectivity across integrated systems. This holistic approach to observability allows businesses to maintain high availability and superior user experiences.

Key Features:

- Automatic discovery and monitoring of MuleSoft Application/API.
- Real-time performance metrics (response times, error rates, etc.).
- Root cause analysis using AI-driven insights.
- Integration with Anypoint Platform for deeper visibility.
- Monitor APIs from your mobile

How Does Integration Work with MuleSoft?

Dynatrace can collect various metrics from MuleSoft Server. In order to get the metrics, we need to install OneAgent on the server. However, it is only possible in the case of On-Prem and RTF based MuleSoft deployment model. It is not possible to install OneAgent in CloudHub, because it is Integration Platform as a Service and fully managed by MuleSoft. In such cases, Dynatrace uses ActiveGate to call Anypoint Platform API and get the metrices available on UI. Not only this, we can monitor any application using either OneAgent or ActiveGate. Let's see the high-level architecture:

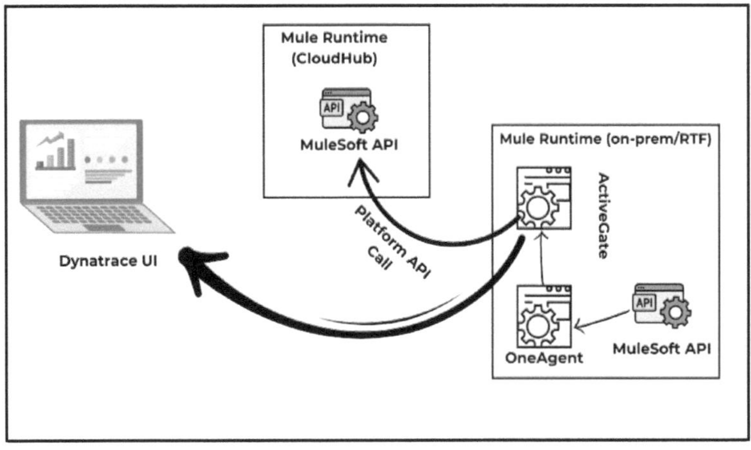

Figure 4.2 - External Monitoring via Dynatrace

- Configuration in MuleSoft Anypoint Platform to configure Dynatrace for MuleSoft external monitoring, follow these steps:

  - Navigate to Access Management

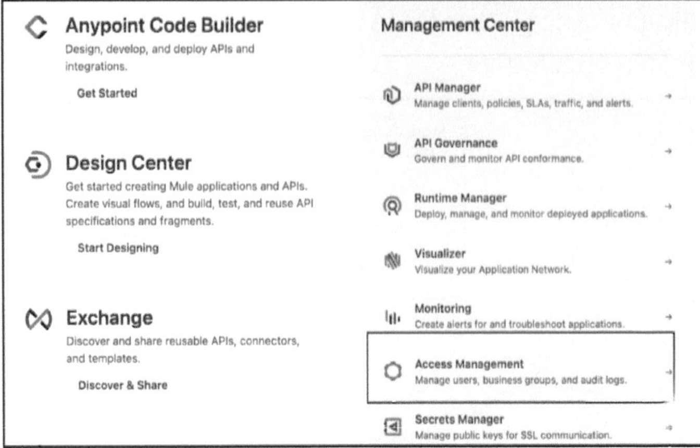

Figure 4.3 - Access Management

- Create Connected App

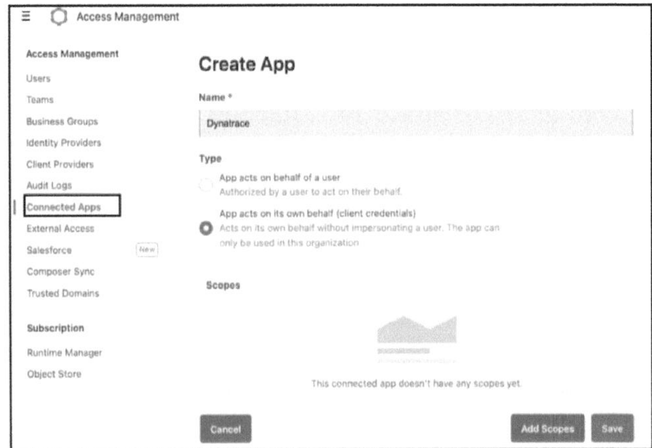

Figure 4.4 - Conected Apps

- Add Scopes. Selected appropriate scope for monitoring

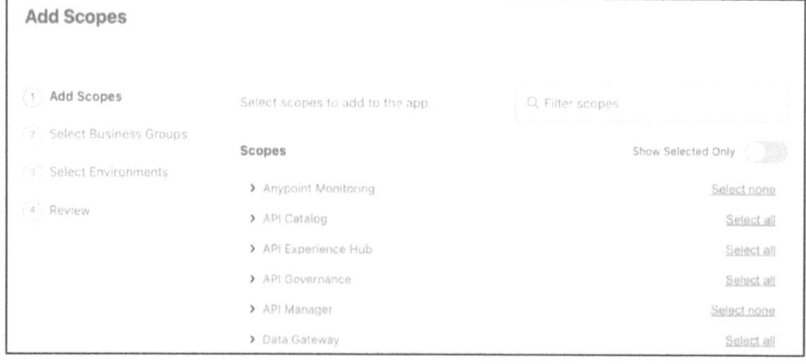

Figure 4.5 - Add Scopes

- Click Next and select Business Group
- Select environment and click next
- Review and click on add scope
- Click on save
- Copy Client and Client Secret and keep it safe. These credentials will be required while setting up Dynatrace.

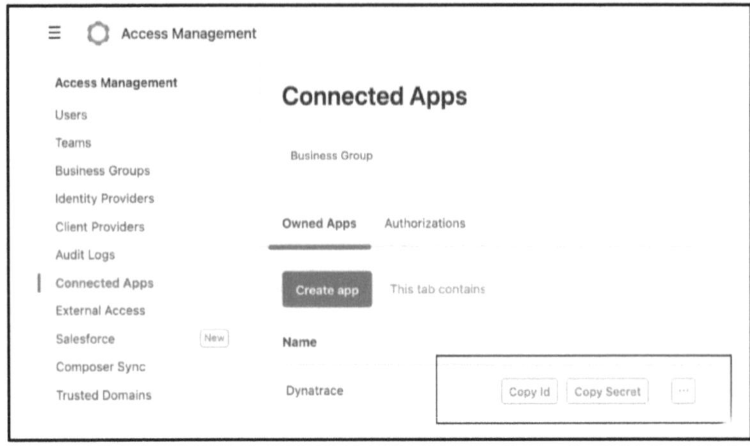

Figure 4.6 - Connected App Credentials

If MuleSoft is deployed on-premise, install Dynatrace OneAgent on the MuleSoft runtime server or Virtual Machine. Kindly refer to https://docs.dynatrace.com for installation of ActiveGateway and OneAgent.

- Register on Dynatrace.com SaaS Portal.
- Generate PaaS Token. This Token is required to complete installation. To generate the PaaS token, navigate to Settings > Integration > Dynatrace API, click "Generate new token”
- Download the Dynatrace ActiveAgent and install it.
- Download the Dynatrace OneAgent installer from the DynatraceSaaS portal. Ensure that you are downloading right installer as per your server OS and CPU architecture.
- Run the installer, Add the PaaS Token and complete installation.
- For example :

- Linux ARM - ARM64 (AARch64) including AWS Graviton processors
- PowerPC (BE) - 64-bit PowerPC
- PowerPC (LE) - 64-bit PowerPC
- s390 - 64-bit IBM Z mainframe
- x86-64 - 64-bit Intel/AMD

- If we are using Dynatrace SaaS portal, Environment ActiveGateway must be installed.
- Ensure that OneAgent and ActiveGateway is up and running
- Now to monitor MuleSoft CloudHub, Open Dynatrace UI, under the extensions on the left menu, select MuleSoft CloudHub.
- Add the monitoring configuration, including MuleSoft URL client id and client secret obtained earlier in MuleSoft configuration section. Frequency is the key which will decide how frequently data has to be collected.

> There are different URLs for MuleSoft Anypoint Platform. It varies according to Europe region, government cloud etc.
>
> - https://anypoint.mulesoft.com
> - https://eu1.anypoint.mulesoft.com
> - https://gov.anypoint.mulesoft.com

- Dynatrace will now start monitoring the MuleSoft application automatically.

Anypoint logs can also be ingested to Dynatrace and it can be presented on the dashboard.

Additionally alert rules can be configured on Daynatrace dashboard. For more details please refer to official documentation of Dyantrace.

AWS CloudWatch for Monitoring

Effective application logging is a critical component of any software development project. No matter how well-designed a system is, unexpected issues can arise in a production environment. When problems occur, a well-structured logging strategy becomes invaluable, providing a detailed record of system activities, error occurrences, and key events. These logs serve as a roadmap for diagnosing issues and ensuring smooth application performance.A comprehensive logging framework captures essential data, including system messages, warnings, and error reports. This information helps developers and support teams identify patterns, troubleshoot failures, and optimize system reliability. By leveraging structured and meaningful logs, organizations can enhance application monitoring, improve debugging efficiency, and maintain a robust, high-performing software ecosystem.

Amazon CloudWatch serves as a powerful tool for tracking, managing, and retrieving log data across various applications, systems, and AWS services. It provides a centralized platform where logs from different sources are aggregated, ensuring seamless monitoring and visibility into operational performance. With its highly scalable infrastructure, CloudWatch simplifies log management by offering a streamlined approach to handling large volumes of data efficiently. This service allows users to search for specific error codes, identify recurring patterns, and apply filters to isolate critical information. Additionally, CloudWatch supports secure log archiving, enabling long-term storage for auditing or future analysis. By leveraging its capabilities, businesses can gain deeper insights, troubleshoot issues effectively, and enhance overall system reliability.

CloudWatch enables you to gather and monitor all your API/Applicaiton performance and operational data, consolidating logs and metrics into a unified platform for seamless access and analysis.

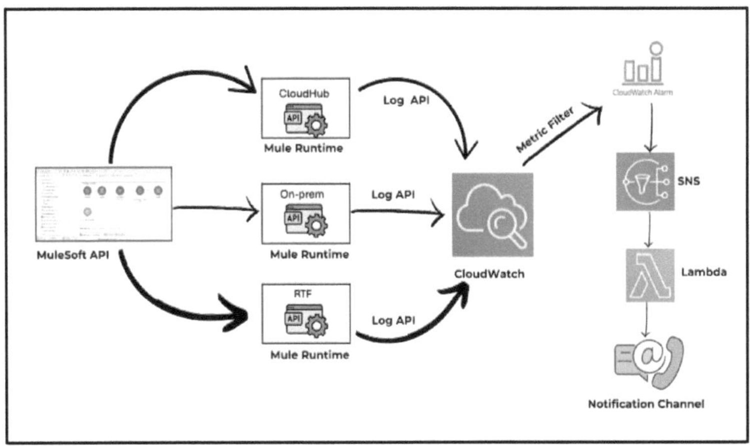

Figure 4.7 - CloudWatch Architecture

AWS CloudWatch enables real-time observability of MuleSoft APIs and integrations. By collecting and analysing metrics, logs, and events, CloudWatch helps teams gain insights into API performance, latency, and error rates. It allows businesses to set up custom dashboards, track API health, and configure alarms to detect anomalies. This proactive approach ensures that any performance degradation or failures are identified and addressed before they impact users.

Integrating MuleSoft APIs with AWS CloudWatch enhances operational efficiency by automating monitoring and response mechanisms. CloudWatch can trigger automated actions through AWS Lambda, SNS, or other AWS services to handle incidents dynamically. With built-in scalability and seamless integration with other AWS tools, CloudWatch provides a comprehensive monitoring solution that helps organizations maintain high availability, optimize resource utilization, and improve the overall resilience of their MuleSoft-powered applications.

Forwarding MuleSoft CloudHub Application/API Logs to AWS CloudWatch

AWS Configuration

To enable log forwarding from Anypoint Monitoring to CloudWatch, following configuration details are required:

- logGroup
- logStream
- region
- accessKey
- secretKey

To get these follow the steps provided below:

- Login to AWS console , Search for CloudWatch and click on it.
- Select logs >log group.

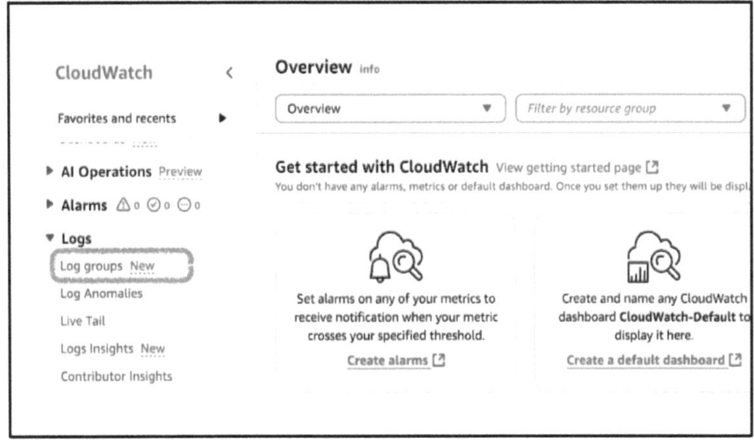

Figure 4.8 – CloudWatch Config

- Click on create log group, enter log group name. Give a name to it.

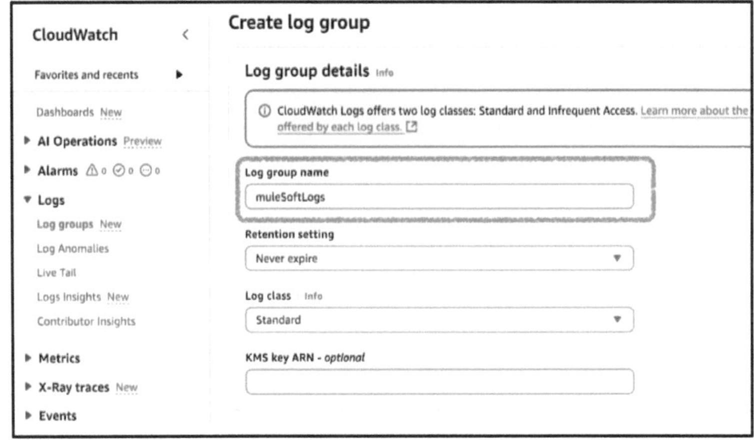

Figure 4.9 - Create Log groups

- Click on log group.

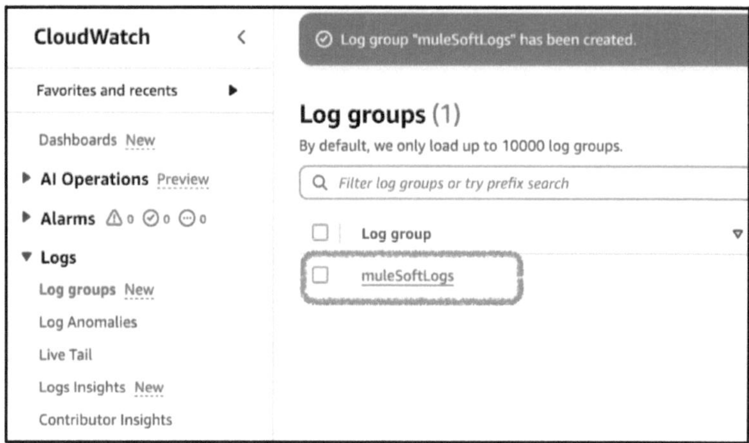

Figure 4.10 - Created Log Groups

- Create log stream. Give a name to it. For example muleSoftLogStream.

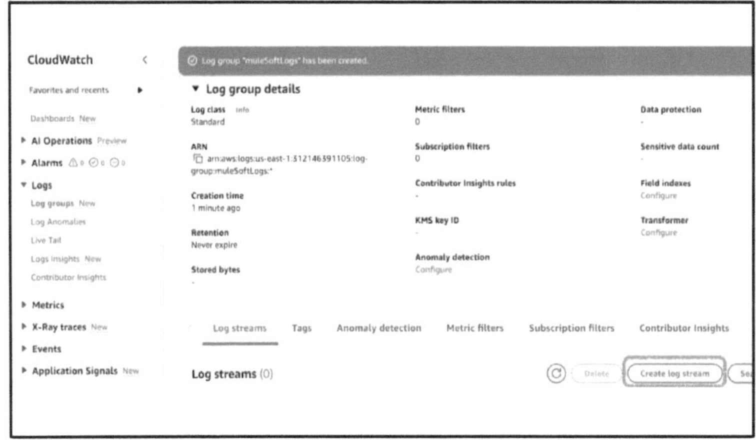

Figure 4.11 - Log Stream

- Navigate to IAM and create users

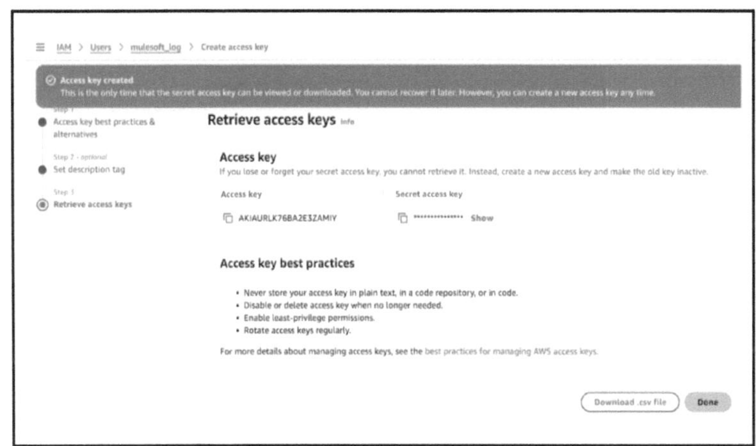

Figure 4.12 - Create Users

- Create IAM accessKey and secretAccessKey

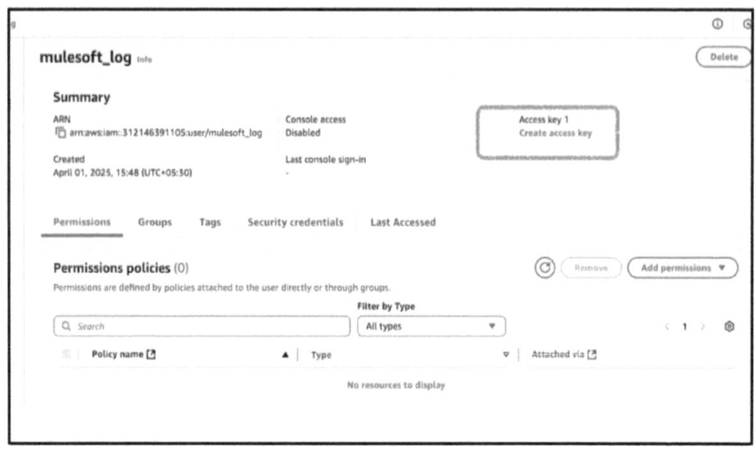

Figure 4.13 - Create Access Key

- Copy these details and save it in vault or secure location

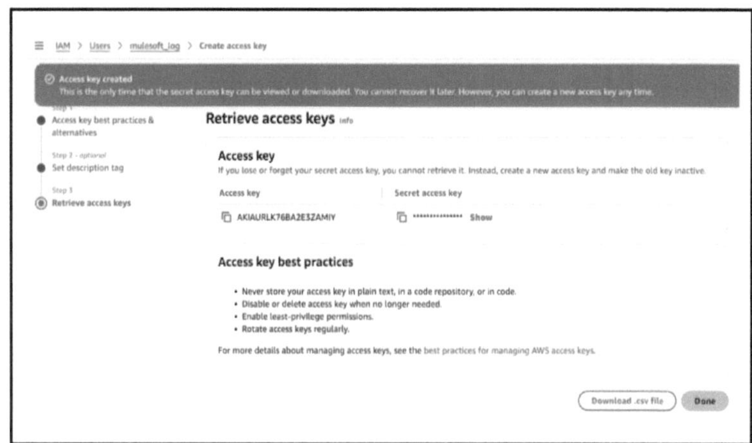

Figure 4.14 – Generated Access Key

MuleSoft Configuration

- Follow the steps provided below, we need to add following dependencies in the API POM file.

```
<dependency>
     <groupId>com.kdgregory.logging</groupId>
       <artifactId>log4j2-aws-appenders</artifactId>
       <version>2.4.1</version>
</dependency>
<dependency>
<groupId>com.amazonaws</groupId>
<artifactId>aws-java-sdk-logs</artifactId>
<version>1.12.293</version>
</dependency>
```

- Add the required configuration packages, appenders, and loggers in the log4j.xml.Configure the MuleSoft Application to log to the appender within log4j.xml.

```
<Configuration status="INFO" name="cloudhub"
packages="com.mulesoft.ch.logging.appender,com.kdgregory.
log4j2.aws">

<Appenders>
   .......
<CloudWatchAppender name="CLOUDWATCH">
          <logGroup><logGroupName></logGroup>
          <logStream><LogStreamName></logStream>
           <rotationMode>daily</rotationMode>
           <PatternLayout
        pattern="[%d{yyyy-MM-dd HH:mm:ss.SSS}] %-5p
    [%t] %c - %m%n" />
```

```
</CloudWatchAppender>
<AsyncRoot level="INFO">
.......
   <AppenderRef ref="CLOUDWATCH" />
   <AppenderRef ref="CLOUDHUB"/>
.......
</AsyncRoot>
</Loggers>
```

- Setup the following properties from Runtime Manager UI. There are certain parameters that AWS packages would require to be initialized before they can be executed. The authentication parameters are detailed in the link.

```
# Runtime Manager Property configuration for CloudHub

aws.region=<aws_region_example_us-east-1>
aws.accessKeyId=<iam_user_access_key>
aws.secretKey=<iam_user_secret_key>
```

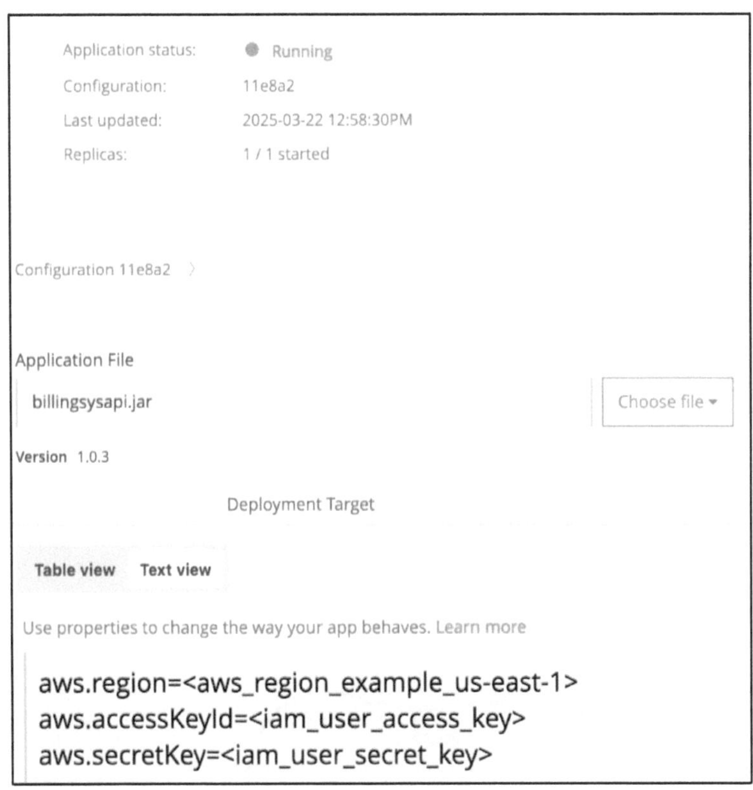

Figure 4.15 - Runtim Manager Config

- After relaunching the Mule CloudHub application with recommended changes, the Cloudhub Application/API will be able to push logs to AWS cloudwatch in the corresponding logging group and stream. For

Application/API deployed on On-prem, we must update the following configuration

```
# Custom AWS Cloudwatch Configurations
wrapper.java.additional.23=-Daws.region=XXXX
wrapper.java.additional.24=-Daws.secretKey=YYYY
wrapper.java.additional.25=-Daws.accessKeyId=ZZZZ
```

Splunk Monitoring

Splunk is a robust data analytics platform designed for real-time monitoring, searching, and visualization of machine-generated data. It efficiently captures, indexes, and correlates data, transforming it into actionable insights through interactive dashboards, alerts, and reports. By providing centralized access to critical information, Splunk enables organizations to diagnose issues quickly and optimize system performance.

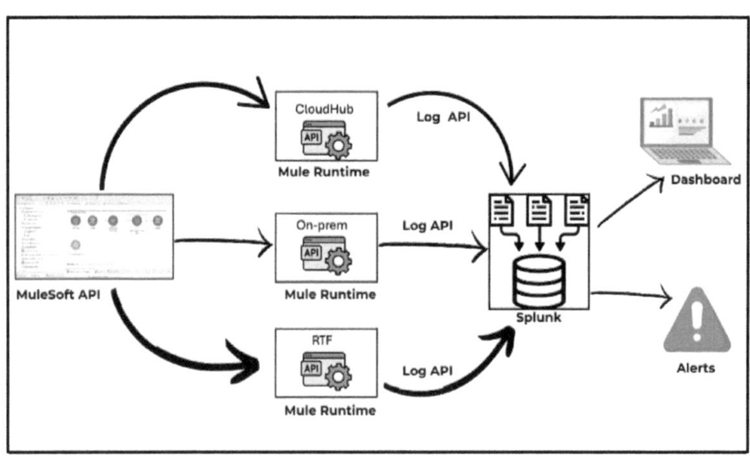

Figure 4.16 - Splunk Monitroing Architecture

MuleSoft, as an integration platform, generates logs and events while processing data. Splunk seamlessly collects and analyzes these logs, offering deep visibility into MuleSoft's operational performance. This integration is invaluable for proactive monitoring and troubleshooting, helping teams swiftly identify and resolve issues. With real-time alerting capabilities, Splunk ensures that any anomalies or disruptions in MuleSoft integrations are detected early, minimizing downtime and ensuring seamless business operations. In order to make this log ingestion work, configuration in Splunk and MuleSoft will be required:

Splunk Configuration

- Login to Splunk
- Go to Settng > Data Input

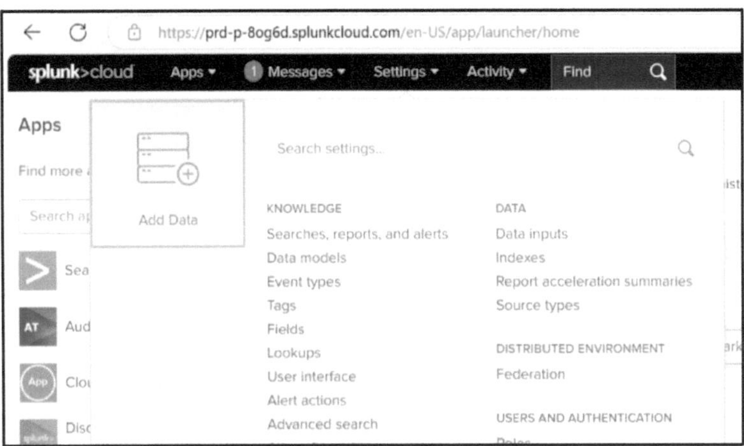

Figure 4.17 - Data Input

- Click on HTTP Event Collector

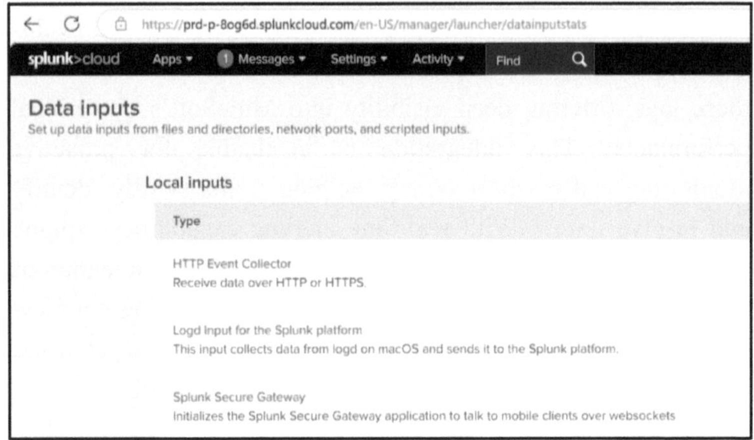

Figure 4.18 - HTTP Event Collector

- Click on New Token

Figure 4.19 -New Token

- Provide Name for HTTP Event Collector and click on Next. I have given name as "AnypointLogCollector"

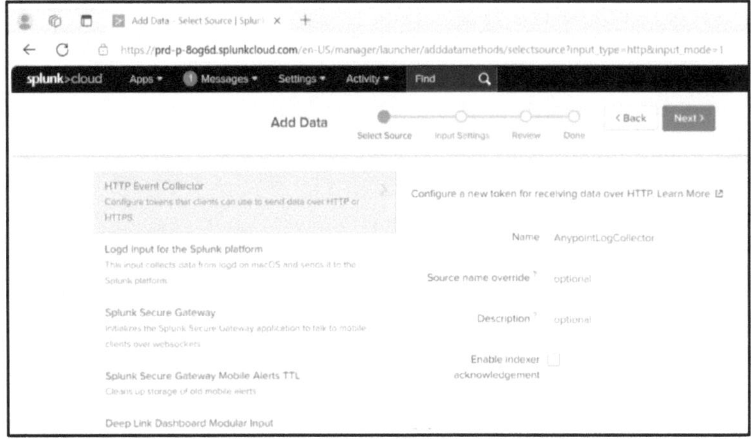

Figure 4.20 - HTTP Event Collector Config

- Click on Select and from drop down select log4j. Click on Review

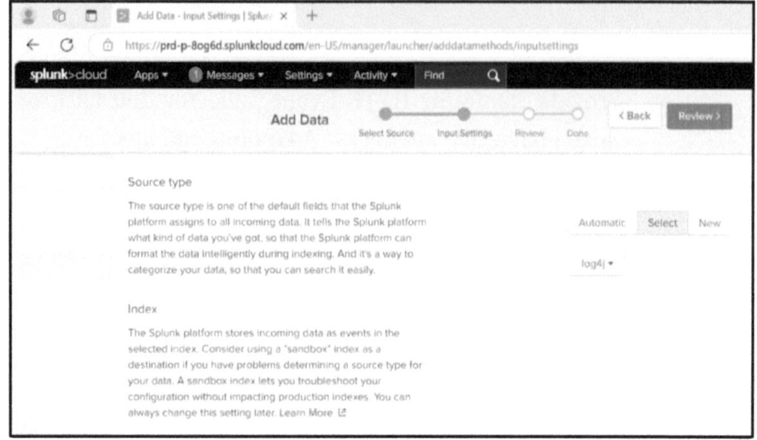

Figure 4.21 - Review Screen

- Click on Submit

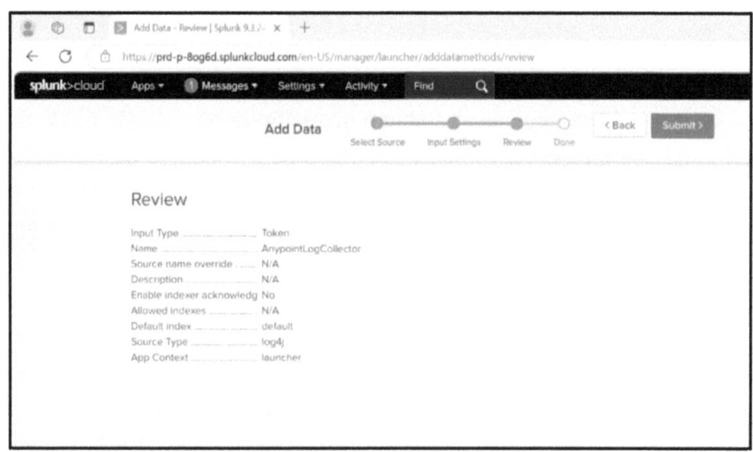

Figure 4.22 - Submit Screen

- Token is created, Copy it and keep it in a Vault or at secure place.

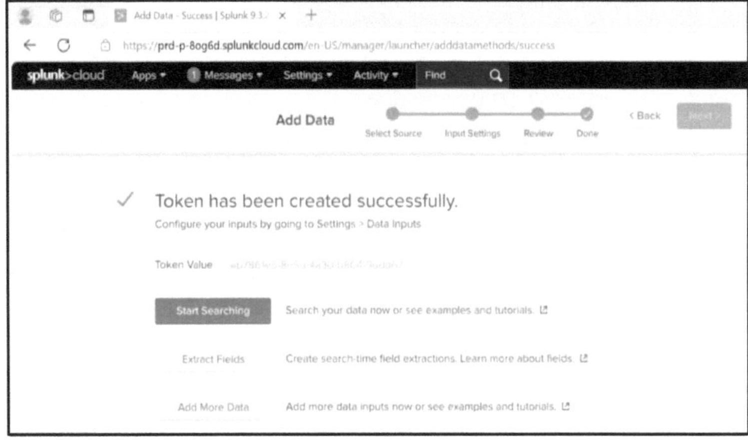

Figure 4.23 - Successful Token Creation

We are done with Splunk Configuration. We will move to MuleSoft Specific Configuration.

MuleSoft Configuration

- Add folloing dependencies in your API/Application POM file.

```
<dependency>
  <groupId>com.splunk.logging</groupId>
  <artifactId>splunk-library-javalogging</artifactId>
  <version>1.7.3</version>
 </dependency>
```

```
<dependency>
 <groupId>org.apache.logging.log4j</groupId>
 <artifactId>log4j-core</artifactId>
 <version>2.10.0</version>
</dependency>
<dependency>
 <groupId>org.apache.logging.log4j</groupId>
 <artifactId>log4j-api</artifactId>
 <version>2.10.0</version>
</dependency>
```

- Add below repository in your API/Application POM file.

```
<repository>
  <id>splunk-artifactory</id>
  <name>Splunk                          Releases</name>
  <url>http://splunk.jfrog.io/splunk/ext-releases-
local</url>
 </repository>
```

- Configure Appender in Log4j file in your Application/API code. You will find it under respurces section. Add the http appender as provided below

```
<Http name="Splunk"
url="http://host:port/services/collector/raw" >
<Property name="Token" value=
"Splunk 5ed04a2c-8221-45e9-9708-7d7b710b0fd7">
</Property>
<PatternLayout pattern="
[%d{MM-dd HH:mm:ss}] %-5p %c{1} [%t]:
%m%n"></PatternLayout>
</Http>
```

- Configure the MuleSoft Application to log to the appender within log4j.xml.

```
<AsyncRoot level="INFO">
<AppenderRef ref="CLOUDHUB"/>
<AppenderRef ref="Splunk"/>
</AsyncRoot>
```

- Next step is disable your CloudHub logs. Once it is done, your deployed application will start sending the log to Splunk. You can search the log in Splunk under Apps> Search & Reporting

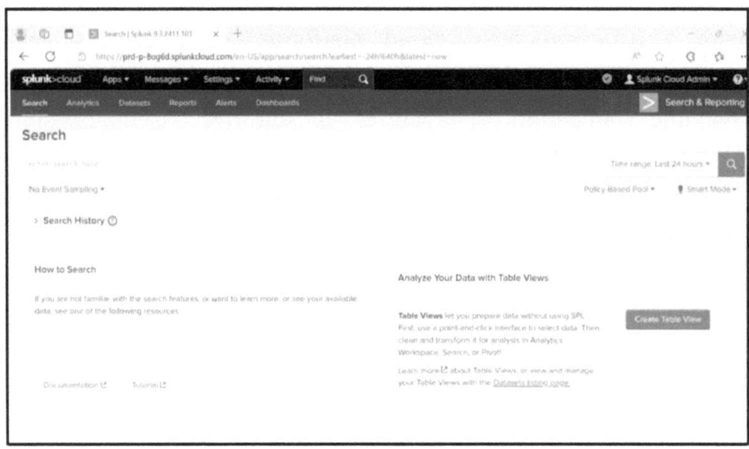

Figure 4.24 - Search Screen

New Relic Monitoring

New Relic Application Performance Monitoring (APM) is a powerful observability tool designed to help businesses monitor, troubleshoot, and optimize the performance of their applications in real time. It provides deep insights into application behavior, infrastructure health, and user experience, enabling organizations to proactively address performance issues before they impact end users.

New Relic APM works by collecting and analyzing application telemetry data, including response times, transaction traces, error rates, and database performance.With its AI-driven anomaly detection and distributed tracing capabilities, it helps developers and IT teams pinpoint bottlenecks, slow queries, and problematic code segments. Additionally, New Relic seamlessly integrates with a wide range of cloud platforms, microservices, and containerized environments, making it a valuable tool for modern, dynamic application architectures. Its intuitive dashboards and customizable alerts empower teams to maintain optimal application performance and ensure a seamless digital experience for users.

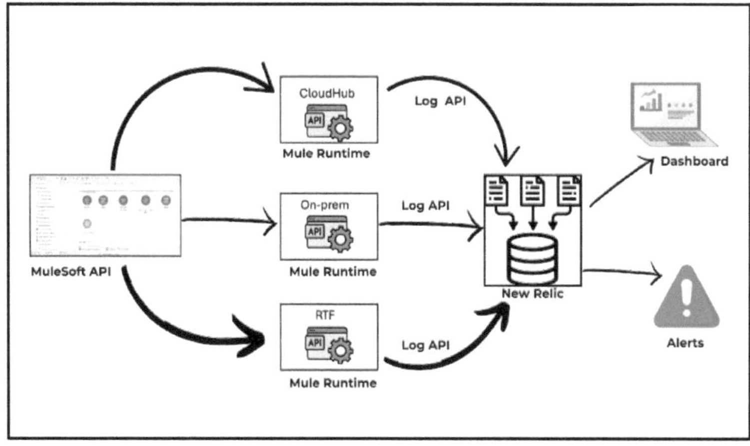

Figure 4.25 - New Relic Architecture

You can ingest and search any volume of MuleSoft CloudHub, On-Prem or RTF Application/API logs. Not only this you can leverge New Relic for cross platform observability also.

To enable MuleSoft Log Management, we can follow the steps provided in the below section.

New Relic Configuration

- Login to New Relic. Go to user and click on API Keys

Figure 4.26 - New Relic Portal

- Click on Create a Keys. Ensure that Key type is **Ingest-License.**

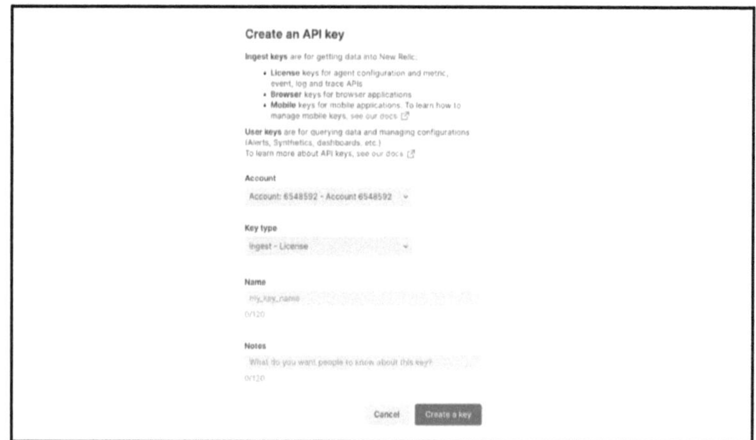

Figure 4.27 API Key

- Copy the key and keep it safe

- Go to https://newrelic.com/instant-observability/logs-api

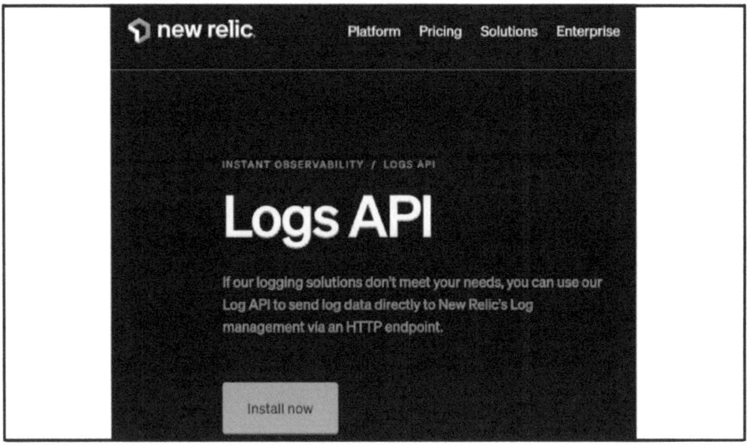

Figure 4.28 Logs API

- Click on Install Now

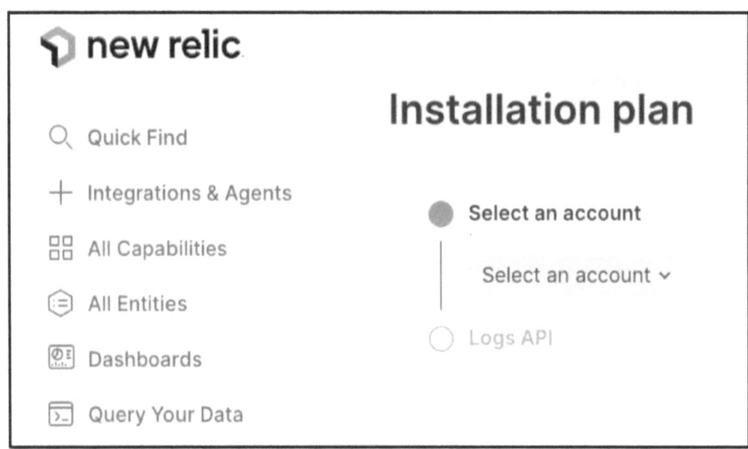

Figure 4.29 Installation Plan

- Select Account and click on Begin Installation

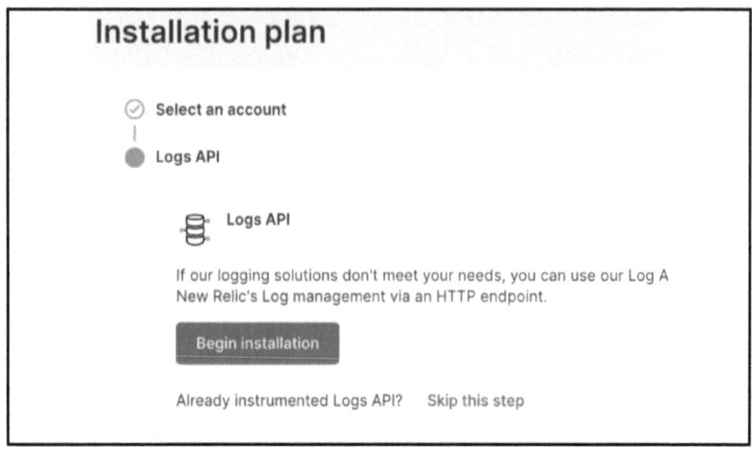

Figure 4.30 Install Screen

- Insert the key created in the begining and click on continue

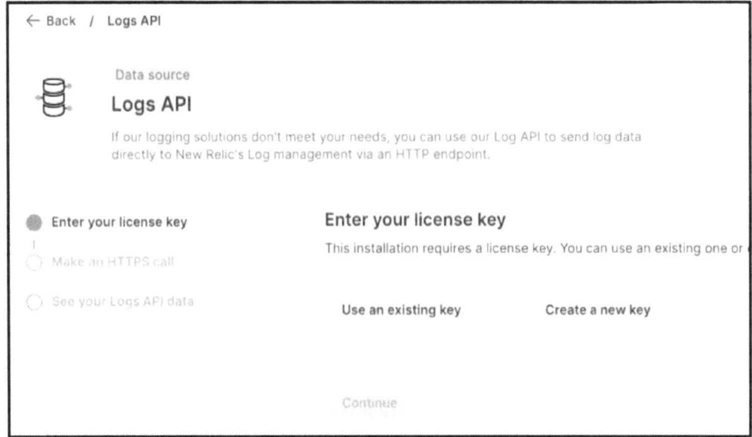

Figure 4.31 - License Key Selection

- Click on use an existing key. Enter the key and click on continue

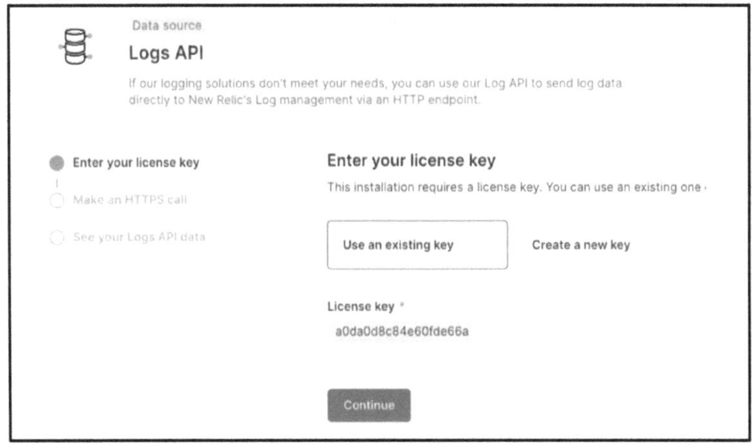

Figure 4.32 - Enter License Key

- You will see log api url

Figure 4.33 - New Relic Log API URL

- Log api url is as follows

United States (US) endpoint: *https://log-api.newrelic.com/log/v1* *European Union (EU) endpoint:* *https://log-api.eu.newrelic.com/log/v1* *FedRAMP endpoint:* *https://gov-log-api.newrelic.com/log/v1*

- We are all set to ingest log in New Relic. There are some parameteres we need to pass while making log api call.

- Api-key must be pass as HTTP header
- It can also be passed as query string also. i.e. https://log-api.newrelic.com/log/v1?Api-Key=YOUR_API_KEY_HERE
- Allowed Content-Type are application/json, json, application/gzip, gzip

MuleSoft API Configuration

MuleSoft API must use HTTP Requester to ingest the log in New Relic. Whatever information you want to ingest in New Relic that you must send as payload on Log API of New Relic.

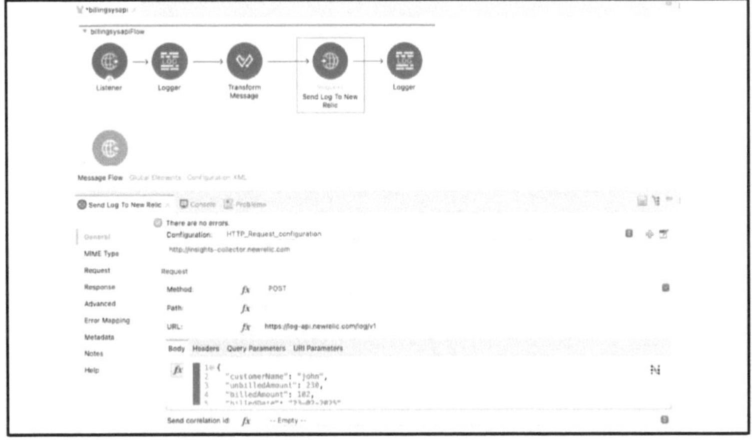

Figure 4.34- AnyPoint Studio Configuration

If you are planning to maintain traeability of transaction passing through MuleSoft API, as well as peripheral applications, you must define a generic JSON message structure. Utilize this JSON message structure to ingest log in New Relic.

For testing purppose you can ingest data using cURL command, postman or any REST Client. For example you can ingest the log using following cURL command:

```
curl -X POST https://log-api.newrelic.com/log/v1 \
-H "Content-Type: application/json" \
-H "Api-Key: <YOUR_LICENSE_KEY>" \
-H "Accept: */*" \
-d '{
"message": "Logs Example",
"logtype": "accesslogs",
"service": "production-service",
"hostname": "production.example.com"
}'
```

- Deploy your api either in CloudHub, On-prem or RTF
- Send some traffic
- BillingSystemAPI will generate some traffic which is a hard coded JSON message

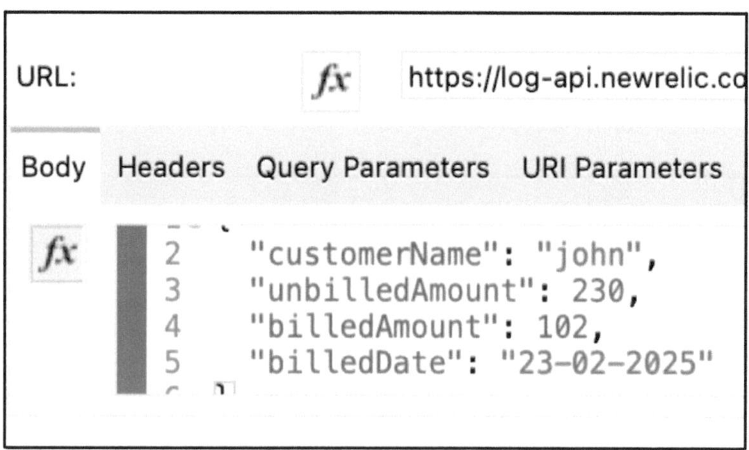

Figure 4.35 - Paylaod Body

- Lets observe the log in New Relic
- Login to New Relic and go to Query Your Data

Figure 4.36 - Query Your Data

- Use New Relic Query Language (NRQL) to search for log. Write the query and click on Run

Figure 4.37 - NRQL

- You can see the result

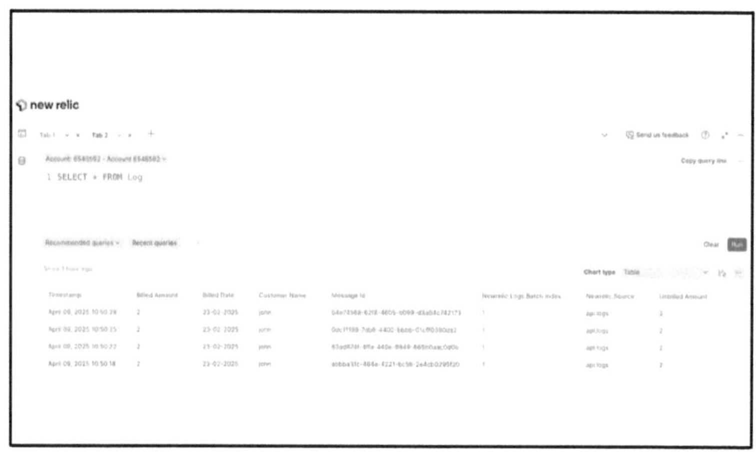

Figure 4.38 - Log Result

- Click on dashboard, you can monitor the metrics on Dashboard

Figure 4.39 - Monitor And Metrics

- You can setup alert condition on the dashboard for proactive monitoring.

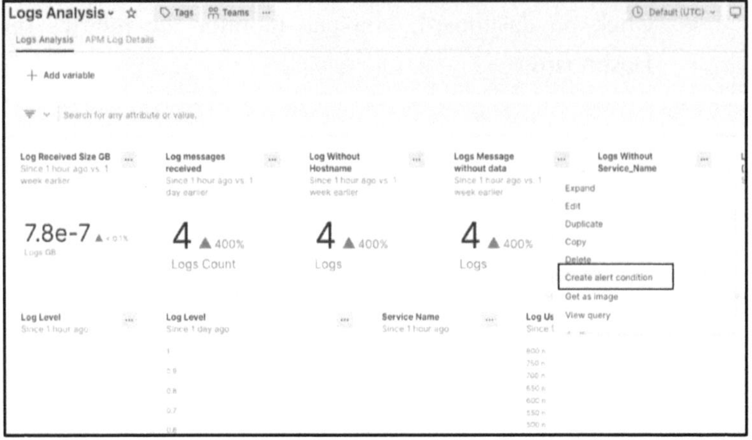

Figure 4.40 - Alert Configuration

- Write alert query. For example if unbilled amount is lessa than 10 Rs., create an alert.

Figure 4.41 - New Relic Query

- Set the alert condition

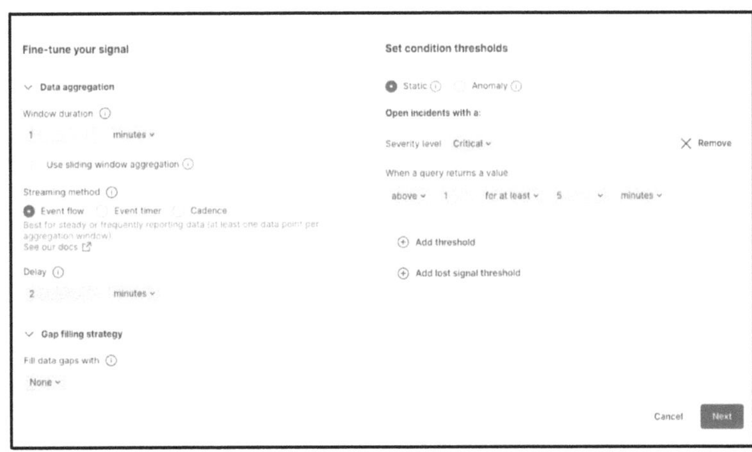

Figure 4.42 - Alert Condition

- Connect alert condition to a policy and click on save and setup notifications

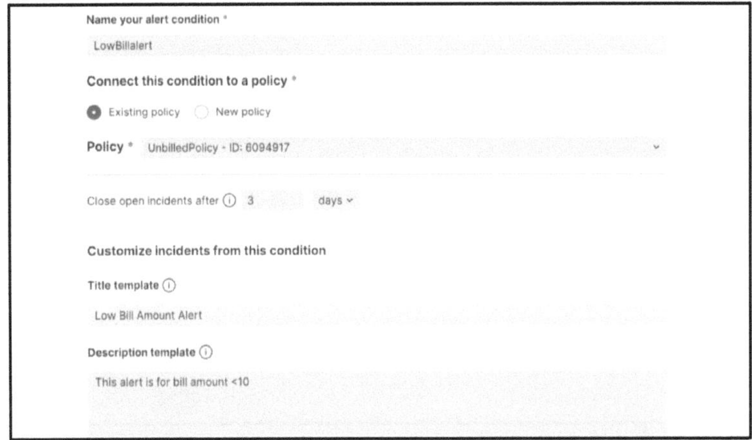

Figure 4.43 - Alert Policy

- Setup notification method for alert. Go to Alerts > Workflows > Add a workflow

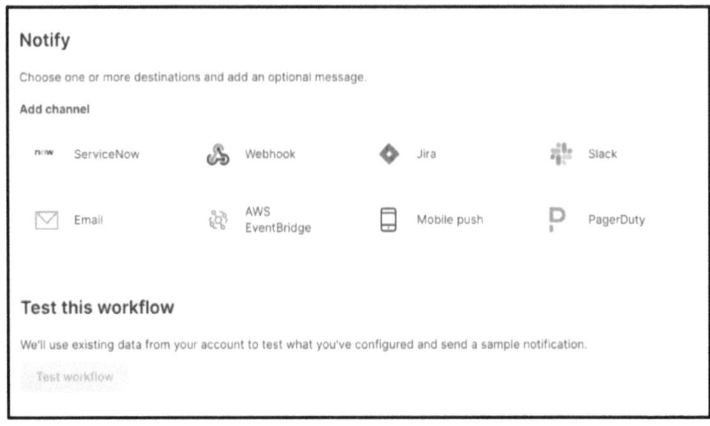

Figure 4.44 – Notification Workflow Config

- For our example, lets setup email notification alert and click save

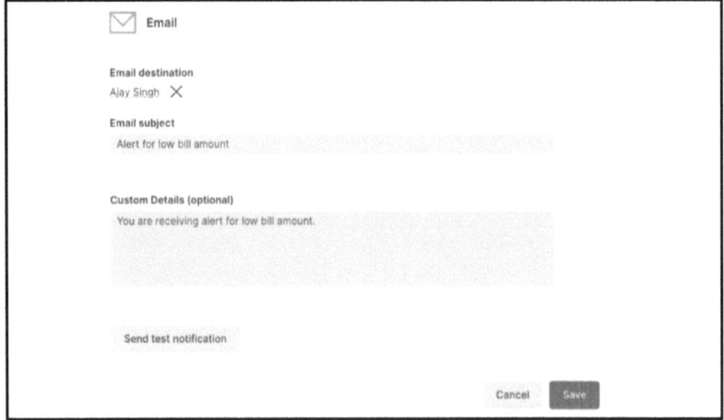

Figure 4.45 – Email Configuration

- Click on activate workflow
- You will receive alert notification as shown below:

Figure 4.46 – Email Alert

Below are some key use cases for New Relic APM:

Real-Time Application Monitoring - New Relic APM continuously tracks application performance metrics such as response times, throughput, error rates, and resource utilization. This helps teams identify bottlenecks in real-time and ensure smooth application operation.

Root Cause Analysis & Troubleshooting - With distributed tracing and error analytics, New Relic APM enables developers to quickly pinpoint the root cause of slowdowns or failures. It provides detailed transaction traces, database queries, and dependency insights to speed up troubleshooting.

Performance Optimization -By analyzing response times and latency across different application layers, New Relic helps teams optimize database queries, improve API response times, and enhance overall application efficiency.

Proactive Alerting & Anomaly Detection - New Relic APM includes AI-powered anomaly detection and customizable alerting mechanisms. It notifies teams of potential performance degradation before end users are affected, allowing for proactive issue resolution.

Cloud & Microservices Monitoring - With support for Kubernetes, serverless applications, and cloud-native architectures, New Relic APM helps organizations monitor the health of microservices, containers, and cloud environments like AWS, Azure, and Google Cloud.

SLA Compliance & Business Impact Analysis -By tracking key performance indicators (KPIs) and Service Level Agreements (SLAs), businesses can ensure their applications meet required standards. New Relic also helps analyze how performance issues impact end-user experience and business outcomes.

Third-Party Dependency Monitoring -New Relic APM tracks external services, APIs, and third-party dependencies, helping organizations identify external factors affecting application performance and reliability.

DevOps & CI/CD Pipeline Optimization- New Relic integrates with DevOps workflows and CI/CD pipelines, providing real-time feedback on application performance after deployments. This ensures that new releases do not introduce unexpected performance issues.

Security & Compliance Monitoring- By monitoring application logs and analyzing anomalies, New Relic can help detect security threats and compliance violations, ensuring adherence to data privacy and security standards.

New Relic APM empowers organizations with deep visibility into application performance, proactive monitoring, and intelligent troubleshooting. It helps developers, DevOps, and IT teams ensure high availability, enhance user experience, and maintain optimal application efficiency in modern cloud and on-premise environments.

ELK Monitoring

The ELK Stack is a powerful suite of open-source tools designed for searching, analyzing, and visualizing log data in real time. It consists of three main components: Elasticsearch, Logstash, and Kibana, which work together to help organizations process large volumes of log data efficiently.

Components of ELK Stack

Elasticsearch - A distributed, RESTful search and analytics engine designed for scalability and speed. It indexes and stores data, enabling powerful search capabilities. Underneath it is document oriented and NoSQL database on the Lucene search engine. It provides RESTFul APIs to search log.

Logstash - A data processing pipeline that collects, transforms, and routes log data from various sources into Elasticsearch. It supports multiple input and output plugins for flexible data ingestion.

Kibana - A visualization tool that provides interactive dashboards and reports based on the indexed data in Elasticsearch. It allows users to analyze trends, detect anomalies, and generate insights.

There is another component for ingesting File data to Elasticsearch and this is called Beats. Beats are lightweight, open-source data shippers that collect and forward data from various sources (like logs, metrics, and network traffic) to Elasticsearch for processing, indexing, and visualization in Kibana

How ELK Stack Helps in Monitoring

Centralized Logging – Aggregates logs from multiple systems, applications, and cloud environments into a single, searchable repository.

Real-Time Analysis – Helps teams detect security threats, monitor API performance, and troubleshoot issues quickly.

Scalability & Flexibility – Supports structured and unstructured data, making it ideal for various monitoring use cases.

Alerting & Visualization – Allows users to set alerts for anomalies and create custom dashboards for better decision-making.

Use Cases of ELK Stack

Application & API Monitoring – Helps track API response times, error rates, and overall system performance.

Security & Compliance – Detects suspicious activities, unauthorized access attempts, and potential breaches.

Infrastructure Monitoring – Monitors server logs, CPU utilization, and system health to prevent failures.

Business Intelligence – Analyzes customer behavior, transaction trends, and operational efficiency.

ELK Stack for MuleSoft API Monitoring

MuleSoft generates logs that can be ingested by Logstash, indexed in Elasticsearch, and visualized in Kibana. This helps in real-time API monitoring, troubleshooting, and performance optimization. Integrating ELK with MuleSoft ensures greater visibility into API interactions, making it easier to proactively detect failures and optimize system health. By leveraging the ELK Stack, organizations can achieve better observability, improved operational efficiency, and faster incident response, ensuring smooth application and API performance. Lets see how it works for MuleSoft API/Application Monitoring. There are multiple options, we will discuss File shipper, Log4j and HTTP plugin based integration.

Option 01 - Using Filebeat for Shipping the Log Files Ingestion:

In this case we have four architectures to achieve this solution. Please note, this solution is not for CloudHub Logs. This is because you cant install Filebeat on CloudHub. In order to ship the log, Filebeat must be installed on the server where Mule Runtime is installed. As CloudHub is Integration Plaform as a Service, it does not allow installation of any external software component/plugins.

There is a workaround of downloading the log files of CloudHub on a server where Filebeat is installed and we can follow any of the four architectures provided further in this section.

We can utilize CloudHub API to download the log files and useing filebeat to ship it to logstash or elasticsearch:

GET https://anypoint.mulesoft.com/cloudhub/api/v2/applications/{domain}/instances/{instanceId}/log-file

curl --location --request GET 'https://anypoint.mulesoft.com/cloudhub/api/v2/applications/my-app-name/instances/{instance-id}/log-file' \ --header 'X-ANYPNT-ENV-ID: 73axxxxx72b' \ --header 'Authorization: Bearer f4ffxxxxebb'

Architecture 01: Filebeat+ Kafka + logstash + elasticsearch + kibana

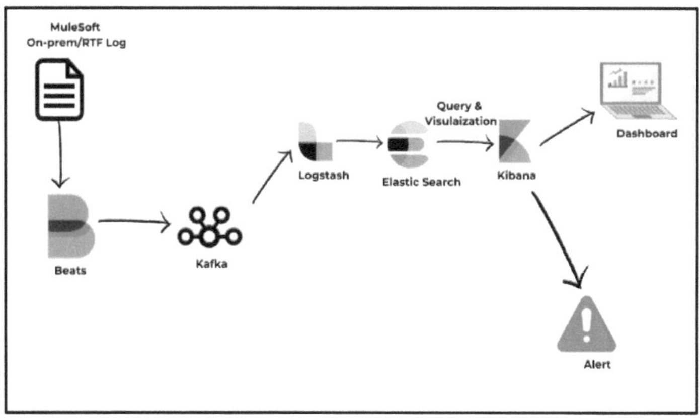

Figure 4.47 - Filebeat + Kafka + logstash + elasticsearch + kibana

Pros:

- This solution provides high scalability, high throughput and fault tolerance.
- This solution is decoupled due to Kafka. Which means log collection and log ingestion are seperate and more realiable.
- Multiple consumers can consume the logs
- Logstash provides filtering, enriching and transformation of log data, if it is not structured.

Cons:

- Kafka consumes Memory, CPU and storage for storing and managing logs, which introduces infrastructure cost.

- Increased latnecy due to addition of kafka layer.
- Kafka configuration overhead and complexity of the solution.

Architecture 02: Filebeat + Kafka + elasticsearch + kibana

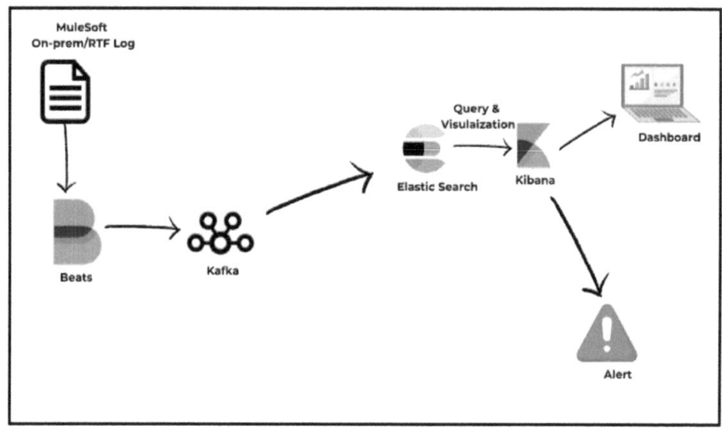

Figure 4.48 - Filebeat + Kafka + elasticsearch + kibana

Pros:

- This solution provides high scalability, high throughput and fault tolerance.
- This solution is decoupled due to Kafka. Which means log collection and log ingestion are seperate and more realiable.
- Multiple consumer can consume the logs
- This solution is good for structured log format. If you are using JSON logger, it is pretty much well structured data. This can be ingested directly to elastic search.

Cons:

- Kafka consumes Memory, CPU and storage for storing and managing logs, which introduces infrastructure cost.
- Increased latnecy due to addition of kafka layer.
- Kafka configuration overhead and complexity of the solution.
- This solution does not provide feature to filter, enrichment or transformation of log data.

Architecture 03: Filebeat + logstash + elasticsearch + kibana

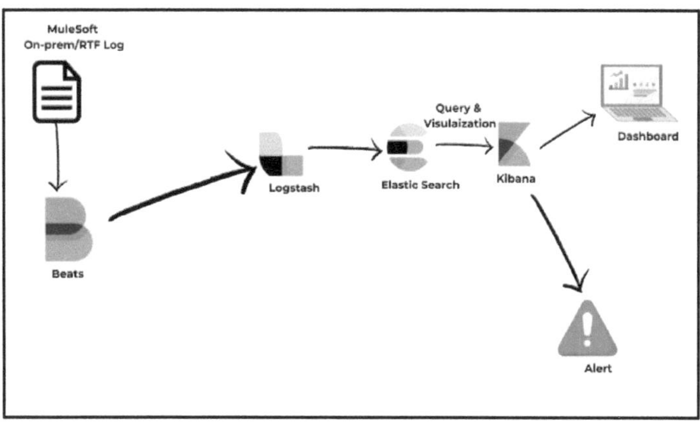

Figure 4.49 - Filebeat + logstash + elasticsearch + kibana

Pros:

- More simple architecture, easier to setup and easier to manage.
- Faster data ingestion as latency due to Kaka is removed.

- Logstash provides filtering, enriching and transformation of log data, if it is not structured.
- As Kafka is not there, less Memory and CPU utilization.

Cons:

- This solution does not provide buffering of log data.
- There is no fault tolernce in this solution.
- Limitations of replaying the log in case of failure.
- This solution is not scalable.

Architecture 04: Filebeat + elasticsearch + kibana

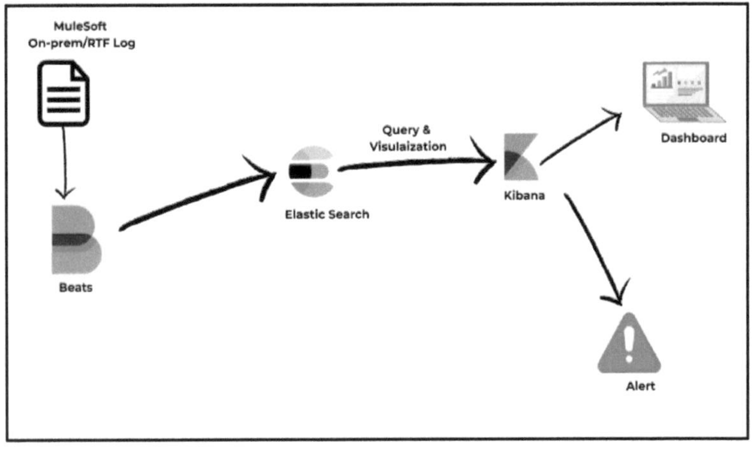

Figure 4.50 - Filebeat + logstash + elasticsearch + kibana

Pros:

- More simple architectture, easier to setup and easier to manage.
- Faster data ingestion as latency due to Kaka is removed.
- **This solution is good for structured log format. If you are using JSON logger, it is pretty much well structured data. This can be ingested directly to elastic search.**
- As Kafka is not there, less Memory and CPU utilization.

Cons:

- This solution does not provide buffering of log data.
- There is no fault tolernce in this solution.
- Limitations of replaying the log in case of failure.
- This solution is not scalable.
- This solution does not provide feature to filter, enrichment or transformation of log data.

You can adopt any architecture based on you requirement. Let's explore Architecture-04, with configuration steps:

Filebeat Configuration: Configure Filebeat for shipping log files from the defined path.

- Navigate to Filebeat.
- Configure input section of config file (filebeat.yml), the path of log to ship. e.g. /var/log/
- This may differ in your case. You need to copy the path where MuleSoft API/Applicaiton logs are getting generated.

```
#======Filebeat inputs =====================

filebeat.inputs:

# Each - is an input. Most options can be set at the input level,
so

# you can use different inputs for various configurations.

# Below are the input-specific configurations.

# filestream is an input for collecting log messages from files.

- type: filestream

# Unique ID among all inputs, an ID is required.

 id: my-filestream-id

# Change to true to enable this input configuration.

enabled: true

# Paths that should be crawled and fetched. Glob based
paths.

paths:

#- /var/log/*.log

/Users/ajaysingh/Documents/Monitoring/ELK/Logs/*.log

#- c:\programdata\elasticsearch\logs\*

# Exclude lines. A list of regular expressions to match. It
drops the lines that are

# matching any regular expression from the list.
```

```
# Line filtering happens after the parsers pipeline. If you would like to filter lines
# before parsers, use include_message parser.
#exclude_lines: ['^DBG']
# Include lines. A list of regular expressions to match. It exports the lines that are
# matching any regular expression from the list.
# Line filtering happens after the parsers pipeline. If you would like to filter lines
# before parsers, use include_message parser.
#include_lines: ['^ERR', '^WARN']
# Exclude files. A list of regular expressions to match. Filebeat drops the files that
# are matching any regular expression from the list. By default, no files are dropped.
#prospector.scanner.exclude_files: ['.gz$']
# Optional additional fields. These fields can be freely picked
# to add additional information to the crawled log files for filtering
#fields:
#  level: debug
#  review: 1
```

- Configure the output section of config file (filebeat.yml).

```
#====Outputs ==========

# Configure what output to use when sending the data collected by the beat.

# --------------------------- Elasticsearch Output ---------

output.elasticsearch:

  # Array of hosts to connect to.

  hosts: ["localhost:9200"]

  # Performance preset - one of "balanced", "throughput", "scale",

  # "latency", or "custom".

  preset: balanced

  # Protocol - either `http` (default) or `https`.

  #protocol: "https"

  # Authentication credentials - either API key or username/password.

  #api_key: "id:api_key"

  #username: "elastic"

  #password: "changeme"
```

- In this section, configure url for elastic search and username, password.
- Start Kibana portal and check the dashboard.

Option 02 - Using http_poller plugin in logstash for log ingestion:

This solution utilizes, CloudHub platform APIs to fetch the log. You can configure Connected Apps and use the client credentials from Connected Apps.

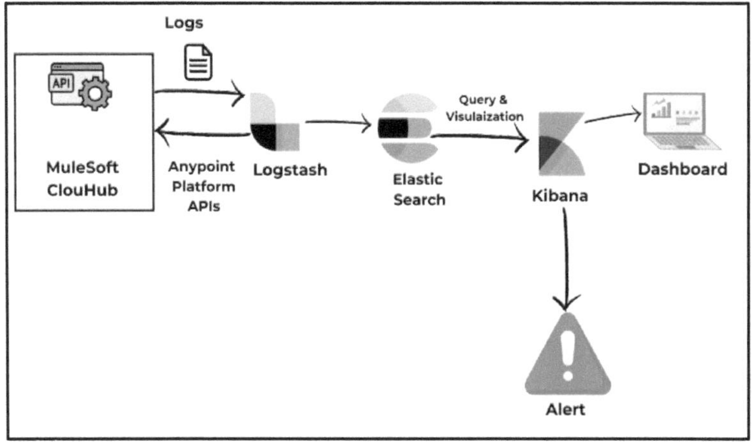

Figure 4.51 - HTTP Poller Plugin

- Navigate to logstash config folder.
- Create a file with name cloudhub_http_poller.conf, add below configuration and save it.

```
input{
http_poller{
urls=>{
authenticate=>{
method=>"post"
url => "https://anypoint.mulesoft.com/accounts/api/
v2/oauth2/token"
body => "grant_type=
client_credentials&client_id=<YOUR_CLIENT_ID>
```

```
&client_secret=<YOUR_CLIENT_SECRET>"
headers=>{
"Content-Type"=>"application/x-www-form-
urlencoded"
}
}
}
request_timeout=>60
schedule => { every => "5m" } #Adjust polling interval
codec=>"json"
metadata_target=>"auth_response"
}
http_poller{
urls=>{
fetch_logs=>{
method=>"get"
url=>
"https://anypoint.mulesoft.com/cloudhub/api/v2/
applications/<DOMAIN>/deployments/
<DEPLOYMENT_ID>/logs"
headers=>{
"Authorization" =>
"Bearer              %{[auth_response][access_token]}"
"Content-Type" =>
"application/json"
}
}
}
request_timeout=>60
schedule=>{every=>"5m"}
codec=>"json"
}
}
filter{
if[message]{
```

```
mutate{
add_field=>{"source"=>"MuleSoft Logs"}
}
}
}
output {
stdout { codec => rubydebug } # Debugging
elasticsearch {
hosts=>["http://localhost:9200"]
index=>"mulesoft-logs"
}
}
```

- Start logstash with the above config file.
- logstash -f /opt/ELK/cloudhub_http_poller.conf
- You can validate logstash server config, if its pointing correctly to elasticsearch. If not then correctly configure it.

Option 03 - Using log4j for log ingestion:

Log4j - We can leverage input plugin of Logstash to take log as input. We can use Log4j, File, or HTTP plugin to ingest data to Logstash.

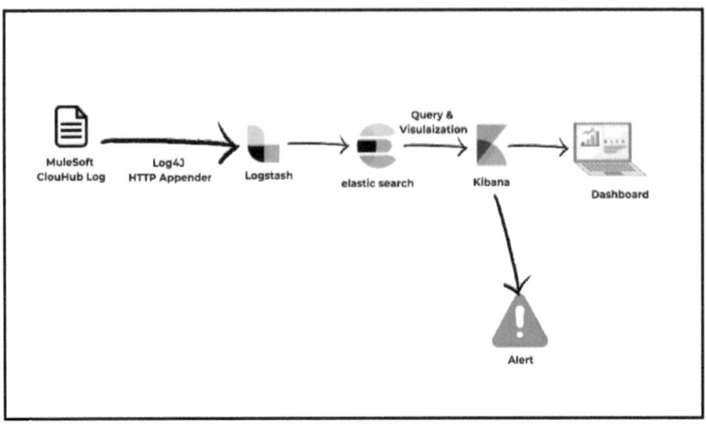

Figure 4.52 - Log4J Appender

- Add the HTTP appender entry to log4j. Configure the MuleSoft Application to log to the appender within log4j.xml.For example:

```
<Http name="ELK" url="${elk.host}:${elk.port}/mule-logs/_doc">
<JsonLayout compact="true" eventEol="true" properties="true"/>
<Property name="kbn-xsrf" value="true"/>
<Property name="Content-Type" value="application/json"/>
<Property name="Authorization" value="{$sys:auth.code}"/>
<PatternLayout pattern="%r [%t] %p %c %x - %m%n" />
</Http>
..........................

<AsyncRoot level="INFO">
  <AppenderRef ref="FILE" />
  <AppenderRef ref="ELK" />
</AsyncRoot>
```

- Deploy the application and disable the CloudHub logs.

Datadog Monitoring

Datadog is a powerful monitoring and analytics platform designed to provide real-time insights into the performance of applications, infrastructure, and cloud environments. It offers comprehensive observability by collecting and analyzing logs, metrics, and traces from various sources, helping teams detect anomalies and troubleshoot issues efficiently. With its AI-driven alerts, dashboards, and automation features, Datadog enables organizations to proactively monitor their systems, ensuring optimal performance and minimal downtime.

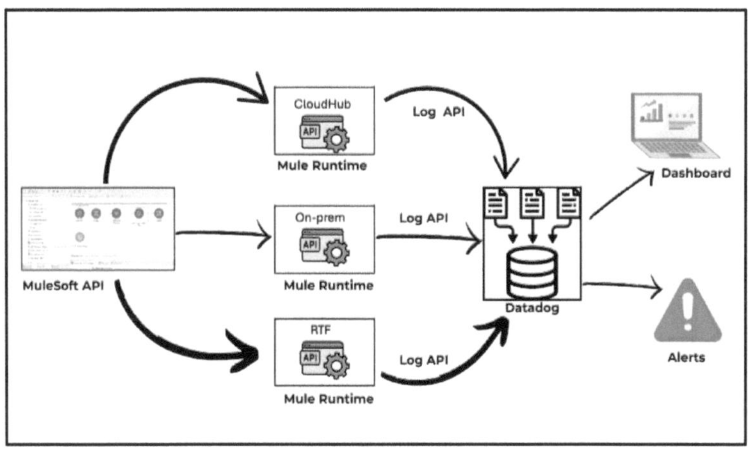

Figure 4.53 - Datadog Log Ingestion Architecture

When it comes to monitoring MuleSoft APIs, Datadog proves to be a valuable tool by tracking API performance, response times, error rates, and infrastructure health. It allows teams to set up customized dashboards to visualize API traffic patterns, detect latency issues, and identify bottlenecks. MuleSoft Logs can be ingested to Datadog and custom dashboard can be created for observability. To forward the logs of MuleSoft APIs to Datadog following configurations are required.

Datadog Configuration:

We will need API Key and log ingestion Datadog url.

- Login to Datadog and get the API Key
- URL will be as follows:

```
https://http-
intake.logs.datadoghq.com/v1/input?host=${sys:host
Name}&amp;ddsource=Mulesoft&amp;service=loggi
ngApp&amp;ddtags=env:Dev&amp;app=
```

- Host, Application or API name and env are the parameter which you need to pass in the url

MuleSoft Configuration:

Modify the log4j file under resources folder of your API/Application. Configure the MuleSoft Application to log to the appender within log4j.xml. Add the http appender as provided below:

```
<Http name="DataDog" url="https://http-
intake.logs.datadoghq.com/v1/input?host=
${sys:hostName}&amp;ddsource=Mulesoft&amp;service
```

```
=loggingApp&amp;ddtags=env:Dev&amp;app=helloWor
ld_myapp">

<Property name="Content-Type"
value="application/json" />

<Property name="DD-API-KEY" value="xxxx" />
<JSONLayout compact="true" eventEol="true"
properties="true" stacktraceAsString="true">
<KeyValuePair key="host" value="${sys:hostName}" />

<KeyValuePair key="apiName"
value="helloWorld_myapp" />

<KeyValuePair key="appName" value="DataDog
Cloudhub POC" />

<KeyValuePair key="apiType" value="sys" />

<KeyValuePair key="ddsource" value="mule" />
<KeyValuePair key="service" value="${sys:dd.service}"
/>
KeyValuePair key="correlationId"
value="$${ctx:correlationId:-}" />
</JSONLayout>
</Http>
```

- Once API is deployed, disable the CloudHub logging. Logs will start flowing to Datadog.
- Configure Monitors for API failures, slow responses, log errors or anyother metrics .
- Set up notifications via Slack, PagerDuty, or email.

5. Shift Left Approach for Monitoring

The shift-left approach to API monitoring enables teams to deliver reliable, high-performing, and secure APIs by identifying and resolving issues early in the development lifecycle. By incorporating monitoring into pre-production environment, teams reduce costs, improve user experience, and ensure API readiness before deployment.

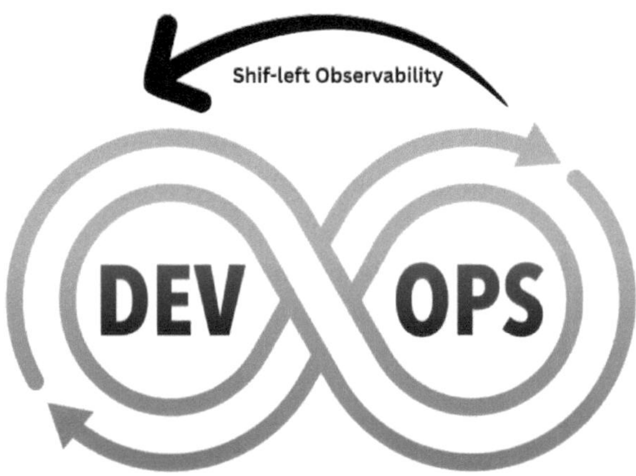

Figure 5.1 - Shift-left approach

The shift-left approach emphasizes integrating API monitoring and performance testing early in the software development lifecycle (SDLC), rather than treating it as an afterthought during production. By focusing on proactive detection of issues during development and pre-production stages, this approach helps ensure API reliability and performance.

Key Principles of the Shift-Left Approach

Early Testing and Monitoring:

Implement API testing and monitoring in development and quality environments.Detect performance bottlenecks, errors, and vulnerabilities before they reach production.

Collaboration Between Teams :

Foster collaboration between developers, testers, and operations teams/support team to address potential issues early. Operations team/support team is the one who encounters the issues on daily basis, debugs the root cause and provides resolutions. Operations team input is very much required early in the development, design and testing phase of APIs.

Proactive Quality Assurance :

Validate API performance (latency, throughput), functionality, and compliance against SLAs during the pre-production phase. It must be validated against production equivalent load. The volumetric data must be captured as contract in solution design at the time of requirement gathering. If there is significant deviation detected in production due to any reason. It must be addressed, temporarily and re-validation against new volumetric data must be performed in quality environment.

Run synthetic monitoring to simulate API usage patterns early in the lifecycle:

It is a proactive approach to monitoring applications, APIs, and services by simulating user interactions or automated API requests. It helps detect performance issues, availability problems, and downtime before real users are affected. It is achieved by Simulating API calls to check response times, error rates, and availability, Testing from different locations to identify regional performance issues.

Benefits of Shift-Left API Observability

Early Detection of Issues:

Identifying and resolving issues (e.g., response time delays, improper error handling) during development, reduces the risk of production failures. During the development phase, it is crucial to proactively identify and address potential issues that could impact the performance and reliability of an application. One of the most common challenges is response time delays, which can lead to slow user experiences and decreased efficiency. By continuously monitoring API interactions, database queries, and application workflows, developers can detect bottlenecks and optimize system performance before deployment. Additionally, identifying improper error handling ensures that the application responds correctly to unexpected inputs or failures, preventing unhandled exceptions and ambiguous error messages that could confuse users or disrupt processes.

By resolving these issues early in the development cycle, teams can significantly reduce the risk of failures occurring in production. Addressing performance and error-handling concerns during testing minimizes downtime, improves system stability, and enhances user satisfaction. Furthermore, proactive debugging helps in maintaining smooth operations post-deployment, reducing the need for emergency fixes and costly patches. This approach not only leads to a more resilient application but also fosters a streamlined and efficient development workflow, allowing teams to focus on innovation rather than troubleshooting avoidable issues.

Reduced Cost of Fixes :

Every bug/incident reported in production environment is costly affair to fix. It consumes effort, time to fix. It directly hits customer satisfaction and monetary losses. Fixing bugs or performance issues earlier is significantly cheaper than addressing them after deployment. Every bug or incident reported in a production environment poses a significant challenge, both in terms of cost and effort. Fixing an issue after deployment requires extensive debugging, testing, and patching, which consumes valuable development resources and delays other critical tasks. Additionally, unexpected system failures or degraded performance can disrupt business operations, leading to downtime that negatively impacts user experience. For customer-facing applications, unresolved bugs can result in frustration, reduced trust in the product, and increased churn rates. Furthermore, in industries where service reliability is paramount, such as finance or healthcare, production incidents can lead to regulatory compliance issues and legal consequences.

Addressing bugs and performance bottlenecks earlier in the development cycle is not only more cost-effective but also ensures a smoother user experience post-deployment. The effort required to fix a defect grows exponentially as it moves from development to production, as late-stage fixes often require code rework, integration testing, and emergency releases. Proactively identifying and resolving issues through rigorous testing, automated monitoring, and code reviews helps organizations avoid costly post-deployment fixes. This approach not only enhances system stability but also protects revenue streams by maintaining high customer satisfaction and minimizing potential financial losses due to service disruptions.

Improved Reliability :

Ensuring that APIs are robust and performant before they are exposed to end-users or third-party integrations is crucial for maintaining reliability and a seamless user experience. A well-designed API should handle various use cases efficiently, including high traffic loads, edge cases, and unexpected inputs, without compromising performance or stability. Rigorous testing methodologies, such as unit testing, load testing, and security assessments, help identify potential weaknesses before deployment. By simulating real-world usage scenarios, developers can fine-tune response times, optimize data handling, and prevent bottlenecks that might otherwise degrade performance. This proactive approach not only enhances API efficiency but also reduces the likelihood of production failures that could negatively impact users.

Beyond internal testing, robust APIs contribute to better scalability and smoother third-party integrations. External developers and business partners rely on APIs to be stable, well-documented, and capable of handling requests without unexpected downtime or errors. Performance optimizations, such as caching strategies, rate limiting, and efficient database queries, ensure that APIs can support large-scale operations while maintaining low latency. By addressing potential issues before public release, organizations can build trust with their users and partners, leading to higher adoption rates, improved customer satisfaction, and long-term success in API-driven ecosystems.

Streamlined Deployment :

Continuous monitoring during the pre-production phase plays a crucial role in minimizing deployment risks and ensuring system stability. By actively tracking API performance, resource utilization, and potential bottlenecks before deployment, teams can proactively address issues that might otherwise lead to failures in production. This approach helps maintain uptime, optimize response times, and prevent unexpected crashes that could impact end-users. Real-time insights gained from monitoring allow developers to fine-tune configurations, adjust server resources, and ensure that APIs can handle expected workloads efficiently. Ultimately, this reduces the risk of post-deployment incidents and minimizes downtime, leading to a smoother transition into production.

For example, consider an API that has undergone rigorous performance testing and optimizations before release. Through pre-production monitoring, the team identifies the required CPU and memory allocation needed to handle peak loads efficiently. By fine-tuning database queries, caching mechanisms, and server configurations, they ensure that the API can process requests smoothly without unnecessary latency or resource exhaustion. When such an API is promoted to the production environment, the likelihood of performance degradation, server crashes, or unexpected resource constraints is significantly reduced. This proactive strategy not only improves reliability but also enhances user experience by ensuring that the API performs optimally under real-world conditions.

How to Implement Shift-Left API Monitoring

Adopt Monitoring Tools :

Use tools like Any point Monitoring, ELK, Data Dog, AWS CloudWatch or New Relic to set up monitoring in pre-production. Setting up monitoring in the pre-production environment is essential for detecting performance issues, optimizing resource utilization, and ensuring application stability before deployment. Tools like Anypoint Monitoring, ELK (Elasticsearch, Logstash, Kibana), Datadog, AWS CloudWatch or New Relic provide comprehensive insights into API and system behavior, helping teams proactively identify bottlenecks and failures. These monitoring tools allow real-time tracking of API requests, response times, memory usage, and error rates, enabling developers to fine-tune configurations before releasing applications into production. By leveraging these solutions, teams can simulate production-like conditions, gain visibility into potential problem areas, and prevent critical issues from affecting end-users.

For instance, **Anypoint Monitoring** offers deep visibility into MuleSoft applications, helping teams track API performance and troubleshoot latency issues. **ELK Stack** enables centralized log management, making it easier to analyze trends and diagnose errors through powerful visualization dashboards. **Datadog**, a cloud-based monitoring platform, provides application performance monitoring (APM), infrastructure tracking, and alerting to ensure seamless operations. By integrating these monitoring tools in the pre-production phase, organizations can establish a proactive approach to incident detection, minimize downtime, and optimize system performance before rolling out changes to production.

Synthetic monitoring:

Integrating **synthetic monitoring** for API validation ensures that APIs function correctly, remain highly available, and meet performance expectations before deployment. **Synthetic monitoring** involves simulating API calls from various geographic locations and tracking response times, error rates, and uptime. This proactive approach helps identify potential issues, such as slow response times, latency spikes, or incorrect API responses, before they impact real users. By continuously running these synthetic tests, teams can gain early insights into API reliability, detect inconsistencies, and address problems before they escalate into production failures. This method is particularly beneficial for external-facing APIs that serve third-party applications, ensuring seamless integration and a smooth user experience.

Automated API tests

Automated API tests play a critical role in validating API functionality and ensuring compliance with expected behaviours. Automated testing frameworks, such as **Postman, SoapUI, or REST Assured**, can execute functional, regression, and performance tests against APIs to verify their stability under various conditions. These tests help validate API responses, authentication mechanisms, and data integrity across different scenarios. By incorporating automated tests into the CI/CD pipeline, teams can catch breaking changes early, enforce consistent API behaviour, and reduce manual testing efforts. Together, synthetic monitoring and automated API validation create a robust quality assurance process, enhancing the reliability and efficiency of API-driven applications.

Integrate with CI/CD Pipelines

Automate API health checks during builds and deployments. Automating API health checks during builds and deployments ensures that APIs remain functional, reliable, and ready for production use. By integrating health checks into the CI/CD pipeline, teams can verify API availability, response times, and correctness in real time before and after deployment. Automated scripts can continuously test endpoints, check authentication mechanisms, validate response structures, and detect potential failures, preventing broken APIs from reaching production. Tools like Postman, Newman, or custom scripts in Python or Bash can be used to execute these health checks at different stages of the build process. This proactive validation minimizes downtime, enhances deployment confidence, and ensures that API consumers, whether internal systems or third-party clients, experience seamless and uninterrupted service.

Trigger alerts or rollbacks for failures in tests or metrics thresholds. A **CI/CD pipeline** must be intelligent enough to trigger alerts or initiate rollbacks whenever test failures or metric thresholds are breached, ensuring system stability and preventing faulty releases from reaching production. By integrating automated monitoring and validation checks, the pipeline can continuously assess API performance, security, and functional correctness. If an API fails functional tests, exceeds latency limits, or violates security policies, the system should automatically notify relevant teams through tools like **Email, PagerDuty, or Slack**. Additionally, an intelligent pipeline should support automated rollback mechanisms, allowing it to revert to the last stable version when a failure is detected. This proactive approach minimizes downtime, reduces the risk of production incidents, and enhances deployment reliability by ensuring that only thoroughly validated code moves forward in the release process.

Automating the validation of **MuleSoft API policies** and their configured parameters ensures that APIs adhere to performance benchmarks and security standards. This process involves automatically checking that policies such as **Rate Limiting, Throttling, Security (OAuth, JWT), and Caching** are correctly implemented and optimized for expected traffic loads. For instance, if performance benchmarking determines that an API can handle **100 requests per second**, the **Rate Limit Policy** should be automatically validated to match this threshold, preventing over-utilization while ensuring optimal service availability. Automation tools can continuously scan API configurations, detect misconfigurations, and enforce compliance with predefined standards. This proactive approach reduces manual errors, enhances API governance, and ensures that API policies remain aligned with business requirements and performance expectations.

Establish Alerting Mechanisms

Configure alerts for metrics like response times, error rates, or SLA violations in staging environments. Configuring alerts for key metrics such as response times, error rates, and SLA violations in staging environments ensures early detection of performance issues before deployment to production. By leveraging monitoring tools like Anypoint Monitoring, ELK, DataDog, teams can set up real-time notifications whenever APIs exceed predefined thresholds. For example, if response time surpasses an acceptable 200ms threshold, or if the error rate spikes beyond 5%, automated alerts can immediately notify developers and operations teams via Slack, PagerDuty, or email notifications. Additionally, SLA (Service Level Agreement) violations, such as downtime exceeding agreed limits, can trigger proactive measures to rectify issues before impacting end-users. These alerts help teams maintain high API reliability, optimize performance tuning, and ensure that only stable and well-tested APIs proceed to production, minimizing the risk of unexpected failures.

Conduct Load and Stress Testing

Test APIs under anticipated load conditions to ensure stability during real-world usage. Testing APIs under anticipated load conditions is crucial to ensure stability and optimal performance during real-world usage. By simulating expected traffic levels using load testing tools like JMeter, Gatling, or Locust, teams can analyze how APIs behave under peak demand. This process helps identify potential bottlenecks, such as high response times, memory leaks, or CPU overloads, which could degrade performance in production. For instance, if an API is expected to handle 500 requests per second, conducting load tests at and beyond this threshold helps validate its resilience and scalability. Additionally, stress testing can determine the system's breaking point and ensure proper failover mechanisms are in place. By proactively optimizing API performance through load balancing, caching strategies, and resource scaling, organizations can prevent unexpected failures, enhance user experience, and meet service-level agreements (SLAs) effectively.

Example of Shift-Left API Monitoring

- Development Phase:
    - Developers write and test APIs using mock services and unit tests.
    - Use tools like Postman or Swagger to validate API responses.
- Integration Testing:
    - Run functional, performance, and security tests in staging.
    - Monitor metrics like response time, error rates, and payload validation.
- CI/CD Pipeline:
    - Atomate the test cases.
    - Automate rollbacks or alerts if thresholds (e.g., latency > 200ms) are breached.
- Pre-Production:

- Conduct synthetic monitoring and simulate traffic to identify potential issues under real-world conditions.

Intelligence in CICD pipeline

One of the examples might be configuring the compute resources based on the expected volume and size of payload and testing it diligently. It should never be left for fine tuning this in production environment. Testing and validating all the business requirements including non-functional requirement and technical error cases. Edge case testing must be performed thoroughly. Integrating intelligence into the CI/CD pipeline is an effective way to implement a shift-left approach, ensuring potential issues are addressed early in the development lifecycle. The pipeline can proactively verify whether essential monitoring alerts—such as traffic, CPU usage, memory consumption, and error rates—are properly configured. By identifying missing alerts at an early stage, it prevents performance and reliability issues from reaching production, thereby enhancing system stability and reducing operational risks.

Furthermore, an intelligent CI/CD pipeline can take automated corrective actions when monitoring configurations are incomplete. If critical alerts are missing, the pipeline can automatically apply the required configurations and execute a test script to validate them. This automation not only improves efficiency but also enforces best practices for observability, ensuring that applications are well-monitored and resilient before being deployed to production environments.

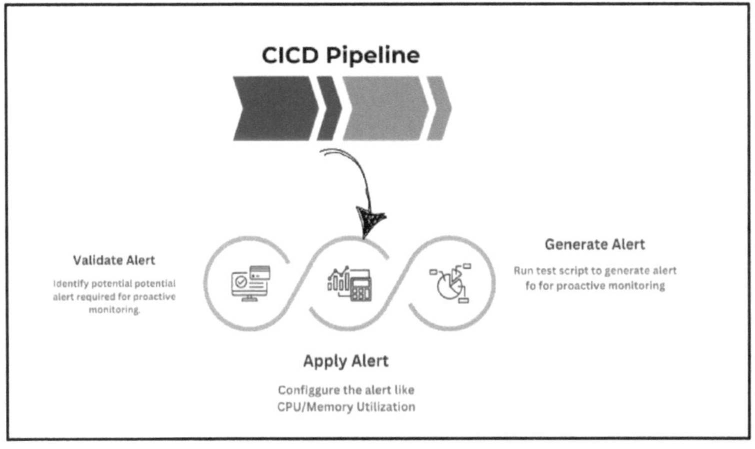

Figure 5.2 - Intelligent CICD Pipeline

Enhancing the CI/CD pipeline by introducing additional steps for monitoring configuration is a straightforward yet powerful approach. By incorporating automated processes to verify, apply, and generate alerts, the pipeline ensures that essential observability mechanisms are in place across all environments. The verification step checks whether predefined alerts—such as monitoring CPU usage, memory consumption, traffic thresholds, and error rates—are correctly configured. If any critical alerts are missing, the pipeline automatically applies the necessary configurations, ensuring that every environment maintains consistent monitoring standards.

This intelligent automation eliminates the risk of human error, which often results in missing or misconfigured alerts. By proactively generating alerts when required, the pipeline guarantees that potential performance or stability issues are detected before they escalate. This approach enhances operational efficiency, reduces manual intervention, and strengthens system reliability. Ultimately, an intelligent pipeline improves incident response times and ensures that teams can confidently deploy applications without overlooking crucial monitoring configurations.

Embedding Intelligence in CICD Pipeline

MuleSoft Anypoint Platform provides a set of APIs that enable automation, monitoring, and management of various operational activities within the platform. These APIs allow organizations to streamline their integration workflows, manage deployed applications, monitor performance, and enforce security policies efficiently. By leveraging these APIs, teams can reduce manual intervention, improve reliability, and enhance overall governance of their API ecosystem. By utilizing these APIs, enterprises can optimize their operational workflows, enhance API observability, and ensure compliance with security policies. Automating operational activities through Anypoint Platform APIs significantly improves efficiency and reduces the risk of manual errors in managing large-scale integration environments.

We have wide variety of Anypoint Platform apis available, However our area of interest is related to the APIs which are helpful in API monitoring and management. We are interested in these APIs because we can consume these to perform many monitoring and management activities programmatically otherwise which we do it manually.

- **Anypoint Access Management API** –This API is used to manage users, roles, and permissions within the Anypoint Platform. It helps automate user provisioning, access control, and security enforcement across different teams.
- **Runtime Manager API** – This API facilitates the deployment, monitoring, and management of Mule applications running in CloudHub or on-premises. It allows operations teams to start, stop, restart applications, retrieve logs, and analyze performance metrics in real-time.

- **Exchange API** – MuleSoft's Exchange API enables users to programmatically publish, retrieve, and manage API assets, templates, and connectors. This is particularly useful for organizations implementing API reuse and governance strategies.
- **API Manager API** – This API helps manage API versions, enforce security policies, apply rate-limiting rules, and analyse traffic patterns. It supports automation of API lifecycle management tasks, reducing the need for manual configurations.
- **Monitoring API** – The Monitoring API provides access to logs, performance metrics, and analytics related to Mule Applications/APIs. It helps in proactive monitoring, enabling teams to detect anomalies and resolve performance bottlenecks efficiently.
- **CloudHub API** – This API allows developers and operations teams to manage CloudHub deployments, scale worker instances, and configure environment-specific properties programmatically.

MuleSoft Developer Portal is a centralized hub where developers can access a wide range of Anypoint Platform APIs to automate and manage various integration and operational tasks. It provides comprehensive documentation, interactive API references, and SDKs to help users integrate with Access Management, Runtime Manager, API Manager, Monitoring, Exchange, and CloudHub APIs seamlessly. The portal enables organizations to leverage these APIs for tasks such as user management, application deployment, API governance, and real-time monitoring, enhancing automation and efficiency. With built-in security, role-based access controls, and collaboration features, the MuleSoft Developer Portal empowers teams to streamline API lifecycle management, enforce best practices, and optimize the performance of their MuleSoft-based integrations.

Figure 5.3 - Developer Portal

You can visit to following link to open developer portal:

https://anypoint.mulesoft.com/exchange/portals/anypoint-platform.

You will find all the Platform management specific apis are well document there.

How to Use Platform APIs

Let's take one example to apply the alerts programmatically. To apply alerts programmatically, it is essential to define the alert types and configurations during the architecture design phase. These alert definitions should be captured as Non-Functional Requirements (NFRs) at an early stage of the API development lifecycle. By incorporating NFRs in the initial design, organizations ensure that critical alerts related to system health, performance, and security are systematically implemented. These NFRs serve as inputs to an automation process that programmatically generates and applies alerts using Anypoint

Platform REST API calls, ensuring consistency, accuracy, and reduced manual intervention.

The process of automating alert configuration follows a structured approach. The first step involves obtaining a bearer token from Anypoint Platform, which is required for authentication and authorization. This can be achieved by making an API call to the Anypoint authentication service. Once authenticated, the automation workflow can proceed with defining alert rules, setting up notification triggers, and applying them to the required environments. This automated alert management not only reduces human error but also enhances monitoring efficiency, ensuring that APIs and integrations remain proactively monitored and well-managed throughout their lifecycle.

- Get bearer token from Anypoint Platform. This can be achieved, by making API call

```
POST https://anypoint.mulesoft.com/accounts/login

Body: { "username":"<USERNAME>",
    password":"<PASSWORD>" }

Response:
    { "access_token":"31ad1f93-32c9-4fde-a786-
    138432eac1de",
    "token_type": "bearer",
    "redirectUrl": "/home/" }
```

- Validate if alert is existing or not. To achieve this use below mentioned API:

```
GET
https://anypoint.mulesoft.com/apiplatform/repository/v2/or
ganizations/{organizationId}/alerts
```

You need to pass {organizationId} value in URI parameter and bearer token as http header.

Response:

{ "total": 45678, "data": [{ "apiVersion": { "name": "BillingSystemAPI", "id": 45678, "apiId": 78600 }, "name": " BillingSystemAPI's Request Count Alert", "severity": "warning", "recipients": [{ "role": "Api Version Owner" }, { "userId": "mtech ", "name": "M Tech", "email": "mtech@mtech.com" }], "period": { "duration": { "count": 1, "weight": "HOURS" }, "repeat": 4 }, "type": "requestCount", "condition": { "aggregate": "count", "operator": "GREATER_THAN", "value": 1000 } }, { "apiVersion": { "name": " BillingSystemAPI", "id": 45678, "apiId": 78600 }, "name": " BillingSystemAPI'sRequest Count Alert", "severity": "warning", "recipients": [{ "role": "Api Version Owner" }, { "userId": " mtech", "name": "M Tech", "email": "mtech@mtech.com" }], "period": { "duration": { "count": 1, "weight": "HOURS" }, "repeat": 4 }, "type": "requestCount", "condition": { "aggregate": "count", "operator": "GREATER_THAN", "value": 1000 } }] }

- Validate against monitoring critical alerts. If it is missing, follow step below.
- To apply monitoring specific alert, use the following Platform API.

POST
https://anypoint.mulesoft.com/apiplatform/repository/v2/organizations/{organizationId}/alerts

Body:

{ "total": 45678, "data": [{ "apiVersion": { "name": "BillingSystemAPI", "id": 45678, "apiId": 78600 }, "name": " BillingSystemAPI's Request Count Alert", "severity": "warning", "recipients": [{ "role": "Api Version Owner" }, { "userId": "mtech ", "name": "M Tech", "email": "mtech@mtech.com" }], "period": { "duration": { "count": 1, "weight": "HOURS" }, "repeat": 4 }, "type": "requestCount", "condition": { "aggregate": "count", "operator": "GREATER_THAN", "value": 1000 } }, { "apiVersion": { "name": " BillingSystemAPI", "id": 45678, "apiId": 78600 }, "name": " BillingSystemAPI's Request Count Alert", "severity": "warning", "recipients": [{ "role": "Api Version Owner" }, { "userId": " mtech", "name": "M Tech", "email": "mtech@mtech.com" }], "period": { "duration": { "count": 1, "weight": "HOURS" }, "repeat": 4 }, "type": "requestCount", "condition": { "aggregate": "count", "operator": "GREATER_THAN", "value": 1000 } }] }

- Will configure the alert with the details mentioned in the body. Similarly many other monitoring specific APIs can be utilized for embedding intelligence in the CICD pipeline. You can refer to developer portal and select the appropriate API according to your use case.

6. Monitoring Strategies and Best Practices

Monitoring Strategies

A well-designed monitoring strategy provides visibility, control, high availability, optimal performance, proactive issue resolution, and continuous improvement. It encompasses key practices such as real-time monitoring, automated alerts, anomaly detection, performance optimization, and regular auditing, ensuring that APIs operate efficiently and securely while adapting to evolving business needs. Let's explore this in more detail.

Defining Objectives & KPIs

Identify what needs monitoring (e.g., system performance, business operations, security). In another term we can say that definition of scope is very important. APIs are not standalone components; it has many peripheral services including servers. There must be a clear definition of what is in scope and what is out of scope. For example, we deploy MuleSoft APIs using CICD pipeline, whether CICD pipeline will be in scope or out of scope. Another example might be platform where we must draw a line whether server monitoring will be in scope of MuleSoft API monitoring, or it will be managed by different team. This means area of responsibility and scope must be clearly defined and documented.

Set clear Key Performance Indicators (KPIs) aligned with business goals. These KPIs may differ from API to API, hence it must be captured at the time of requirement gathering, architecture and design. There might be some APIs which are mission critical, and API up time must be 100%, high throughput is needed for other APIs. Pre-defined KPIs helps Operations team implement appropriate monitoring strategy to monitor and manage api more efficiently

Choosing the Right Monitoring Tools

Use industry-standard tools (e.g., Datadog, Splunk, Prometheus for IT monitoring; Google Analytics for web analytics). There are wide variety of tools available for Application/API monitoring. Monitoring tool feature must be aligned with our monitoring goals. For example, if we have to monitor alerts from a centralized application, newrelic, datadog or opsgenie are the best fit tool.

Ensure integration with existing systems. Monitoring tool must be procured, keeping in mind that it must have capability of easy integration with other systems also. Now a days most of the monitoring tools comes with wide variety of connector which can be used to plug this into any system which we want to monitor.

Setting Up Alerts & Thresholds

- Define thresholds for acceptable performance. Threshold must be captured as NFR (non-functional requirement) at the time of requirement gathering, architecture and design phase. For example, if traffic spike is observed more than 2 times within 5 min, it must be reported as alert and action must be taken. These values must be captured as NFR, and it must not be set/defined by monitoring team on their own.
- Use automated alerts to notify stakeholders of issues. There might be a case when functional error reporting is needed. This might be required by business user or source system or end system. This type of alert condition must

be taken care at the time design and development and support team should be responsible for configuring the contact details of stakeholders interested in receiving the alert. So that they can take appropriate action in a timely manner.

Incident Response & Resolution

- Have a structured escalation process. We must have Service Level Agreement, escalation matrix in place. There must be clear definition of severity and priority of incidents and its response time.
- Use incident management tools (e.g., PagerDuty, ServiceNow). Incident management is used for improved incident response times, enhanced operational performance. It provides structured approach to incident management. It provides 360 views of issues and incidents. This makes management of incident lifecycle a seamless process.

Continuous Improvement

- Conduct regular reviews of issues encountered. It can be weekly review, monthly review or quarterly review. This review must be performed to find out repetitive patterns for optimization. For example, when you analyse the historical issues, you see significant number of issues related to ssl certificate expiry. Based on this analysis, you must create a generic solution for proactive monitoring of ssl certificates and timely rotation of those certificates to avoid the issues.
- Adjust monitoring parameters as needed. Historical issue analysis can help in fine tuning the monitoring parameters. For example, timeout value, if occurring frequently, can be increased. CPU or Memory utilization threshold can be increased/decreased. Alert condition can be tuned for optimum value.

- Implement feedback loops. End user feedback is also very important to address the pain point. There must be a process defined which can be leveraged by Business Users to provide their feedback. For example, if exchange does not have proper documentation of APIs and business user/analyst raises Request for Information asking about the functionality of apis. This could be avoided if we have well defined api documentation in place.

Best Practices for Effective Monitoring

Keep it Simple – Monitor only what's necessary to avoid data overload. When monitoring APIs, it is crucial to focus only on the most relevant metrics to prevent data overload and ensure efficient analysis. Tracking excessive data points can lead to unnecessary complexity, increased storage costs, and difficulty in identifying critical issues. Instead, organizations should define key performance indicators (KPIs) such as latency, error rates, response times, and request volumes, ensuring that only essential data is collected for performance evaluation. This targeted approach helps in optimizing resource utilization while maintaining a clear and actionable monitoring strategy. By limiting API monitoring to necessary parameters, teams can streamline alerting mechanisms and reduce noise, preventing false alarms and improving response times. Intelligent filtering of monitoring data allows engineers to focus on meaningful trends and anomalies, enabling quicker identification and resolution of potential issues. Additionally, leveraging AI-driven analytics and automation can further refine monitoring practices, ensuring that only high-priority alerts are surfaced while redundant or low-impact data points are minimized. This approach ultimately enhances operational efficiency and improves the overall reliability of API ecosystems.

Setup Automated alert and notification for critical failures - Automating alerts and notifications for critical API failures ensures rapid detection and response, minimizing downtime and potential business impact. By leveraging monitoring tools and AI-driven observability platforms, organizations can define thresholds and failure conditions to trigger alerts in real-time. This proactive approach helps in identifying issues such as high response times, 5xx errors, or API outages and ensures that support teams are notified immediately. Additionally, integrating automated notifications with incident management systems allows for seamless escalation and resolution. Alerts can be configured to notify on-call engineers via email, SMS, or collaboration tools like Slack and Microsoft Teams. This ensures that critical failures are addressed promptly, reducing mean time to resolution (MTTR). AI-driven automation can further enhance this process by categorizing issues, suggesting fixes, and even executing predefined recovery actions to restore API availability.

mplement rate limiting and throttling to prevent unexpected volume- Implementing rate limiting and throttling is essential for maintaining API stability and ensuring fair usage. Rate limiting helps control the number of API requests a client can make within a specific timeframe, preventing excessive or malicious traffic from overwhelming the system. Throttling, on the other hand, slows down API requests once a predefined limit is reached, allowing critical services to remain available while mitigating risks associated with sudden traffic spikes. By enforcing these measures, organizations can protect backend resources, improve performance, and enhance user experience. Properly configured rate limits prevent unexpected surges that could degrade response times or lead to downtime. Additionally, integrating adaptive throttling techniques with AI-driven traffic analysis ensures dynamic adjustments based on real-time demand, further optimizing resource allocation and maintaining system reliability.

Create custom dashboard to get real-time insights of various matrices- Creating a custom dashboard for API monitoring enables real-time visibility into various performance metrics. It provides a centralized view of key indicators such as response times, error rates, traffic volume, and latency trends. By leveraging real-time analytics, teams can identify issues proactively, ensuring APIs operate efficiently and meet SLAs. A well-designed dashboard enhances operational efficiency by enabling quick decision-making based on live data. It allows teams to set up custom alerts, visualize trends, and gain actionable insights into API performance. By integrating AI-driven anomaly detection, organizations can anticipate failures and optimize API health, ensuring a seamless experience for end-users.

Utilize in-built dashboard to get real-time insights of various matrices- Leveraging an in-built dashboard allows organizations to gain real-time insights into various API performance metrics. These dashboards provide a comprehensive view of critical indicators such as response times, error rates, traffic patterns, and system health. With pre-configured visualizations, teams can monitor API behaviour efficiently and identify potential issues before they impact users. By utilizing built-in analytics tools, businesses can enhance operational decision-making and ensure APIs meet performance expectations. These dashboards help track trends, detect anomalies, and generate alerts, allowing proactive troubleshooting. With seamless integration into monitoring frameworks, they empower teams to maintain high availability and optimize API performance effectively.

Automate – AI-driven tools can significantly enhance proactive issue detection by continuously analysing system performance and identifying anomalies before they escalate into critical failures. These tools leverage machine learning algorithms to detect patterns, predict potential issues, and automate responses, ensuring seamless operations. By monitoring real-time data, AI can flag irregularities, reducing downtime and improving overall system reliability. Implementing AI-powered monitoring solutions allows businesses to stay ahead of potential disruptions. These tools can correlate data from various sources, providing actionable insights and alerting teams to potential risks. By automating issue detection and response, organizations can minimize manual intervention, enhance efficiency, and maintain high API availability.

Ensure Scalability – As an organization expands, its monitoring strategy must adapt to accommodate increased complexity, higher traffic, and evolving infrastructure. A static approach to monitoring may not effectively capture new challenges, leading to potential blind spots in performance and security. By continuously refining monitoring techniques, businesses can ensure that they maintain visibility into critical metrics and proactively address emerging issues. Scaling operations requires a flexible and dynamic monitoring strategy that integrates new technologies and methodologies. As workloads grow, leveraging automation, AI-driven insights, and real-time analytics becomes essential to maintain system stability. Regularly reviewing and updating the monitoring framework allows businesses to optimize performance, minimize downtime, and enhance overall operational efficiency.

Establish Accountability – Clearly defining roles for monitoring and response ensures an organized and efficient incident management process. Assigning dedicated team members to oversee specific monitoring tasks helps in detecting anomalies early and addressing potential issues before they escalate. By designating responsibilities, organizations can create a structured approach where individuals or teams specialize in areas such as API performance monitoring, security alerts, or infrastructure health, leading to a more proactive operational environment. In addition to assigning roles, establishing a clear response protocol is essential for quick and effective issue resolution. Defining escalation paths, response timelines, and communication channels ensures that incidents are addressed in a timely manner. With well-defined roles and responsibilities, teams can work collaboratively to mitigate risks, minimize downtime, and maintain overall system reliability.

Regularly Test & Optimize – Regular testing and optimization are essential to maintain an effective API monitoring strategy. Conducting regular audits helps identify potential performance bottlenecks, security vulnerabilities, and inefficiencies. By analysing historical data and monitoring insights, organizations can pinpoint areas that require improvement and ensure their APIs are operating at optimal performance levels. Proactively addressing these issues prevents unexpected failures and enhances overall system reliability. Optimization should be an ongoing process where API monitoring strategies evolve based on real-time data and business needs. Leveraging insights from audits allows teams to refine monitoring parameters, fine-tune alert mechanisms, and enhance API resilience. Continuous improvements not only boost performance but also ensure compliance with service-level agreements (SLAs) and business objectives, leading to a more efficient and scalable API ecosystem.

Validation in CICD pipeline – Integrating validation checks within the CI/CD pipeline is crucial for ensuring API configurations align with the desired monitoring parameters. By embedding automated validation mechanisms, teams can proactively detect discrepancies in API settings before deployment. This approach enhances reliability, prevents misconfigurations, and ensures that monitoring thresholds are consistently enforced across different environments. Intelligent CI/CD pipeline should be capable of scanning API configurations and comparing them with predefined monitoring benchmarks. Automated scripts can validate parameters such as rate limits, logging levels, response time thresholds, and alert mechanisms. If any deviation from the expected values is detected, the pipeline can trigger notifications or halt the deployment process to mitigate potential issues before they impact production systems. Continuous improvement of the CI/CD validation process is essential to keep up with evolving API monitoring needs. By regularly refining the validation rules based on insights from past incidents, organizations can enhance their API governance and observability. This proactive approach not only strengthens API security and performance but also fosters a more resilient and efficient deployment workflow.

Error Handling- Providing descriptive error messages along with error codes is essential for improving the troubleshooting process when MuleSoft API calls fail. Clear and informative error responses help developers and support teams quickly identify the root cause of an issue, whether it's due to incorrect input, authentication failures, or system errors. By including meaningful details in error messages, such as what went wrong and possible solutions, API consumers can resolve issues more efficiently without unnecessary guesswork. In addition to enhancing debugging, structured error handling improves the overall user experience by making API interactions more transparent. Standardizing error messages and codes ensures consistency across all API responses, making it easier to interpret failures and take corrective actions. This approach not only reduces downtime but also strengthens the reliability and maintainability of the API, ultimately leading to a more seamless integration process for end users.

7. AIOps, GenAI & API Observability

Role of Generative AI and Agentic AI in API Observability

Generative AI and Agentic AI are transforming API monitoring and management by enabling intelligent automation, predictive insights, and self-healing capabilities. Generative AI can analyze vast amounts of API logs, generate anomaly reports, and provide recommendations for optimizing performance. By leveraging machine learning models, it can detect patterns in API behavior, forecast potential failures, and suggest improvements for scaling resources efficiently. Additionally, Generative AI can automate documentation generation, ensuring that API specifications remain up-to-date and accessible for developers. Agentic AI takes API management a step further by introducing autonomous decision-making capabilities. Unlike traditional monitoring tools that rely on predefined rules, Agentic AI can proactively adjust configurations, optimize traffic routing, and even trigger rollbacks in case of performance degradation. It continuously learns from real-time data and adapts to changes in API usage patterns, ensuring stability and reliability. Moreover, Agentic AI-driven systems can autonomously handle incident resolution by integrating with alerting tools and taking corrective actions without human intervention, thereby minimizing downtime and enhancing overall system resilience.

Incident remediation Assistant:

Diagnosing API failures and implementing self-healing actions, such as restarting services, scaling infrastructure, or re-routing traffic, are crucial for maintaining system reliability. By leveraging AI-driven monitoring, APIs can automatically detect anomalies, analyze failure patterns, and execute corrective measures in real time. For instance, if an API experiences high latency due to increased traffic, an intelligent system can dynamically allocate additional resources or reroute requests to a healthier instance, ensuring seamless performance. Let's explore a specific use case to understand the practical implementation of this approach.

Use Case 01:

In the given integration, the Billing System API may become unresponsive, causing the Experience API to return a 502 Bad Gateway or Timeout Error. Such failures can disrupt user interactions and degrade service quality. Monitoring logs and performance metrics manually can be time-consuming, often leading to delays in issue resolution. Traditionally, a human support engineer would analyze the logs, identify the root cause, and restart the API to restore functionality. However, this process may take longer, especially if the issue arises outside business hours. An AI-driven agent, on the other hand, can continuously monitor system logs and performance metrics in real-time, detecting anomalies as soon as they occur. Upon identifying an API failure, it can autonomously decide to restart the unresponsive API without human intervention, minimizing downtime and improving overall system reliability. Unlike human engineers, AI agents operate 24/7, ensuring that corrective actions are taken immediately whenever an issue arises. This proactive approach enhances service availability and reduces operational overhead, making API management more efficient.

Use Case 02:

If a 400 Bad Request error is detected in the logs, an AI agent can automatically create a Service Request (SRQ) with relevant details extracted from the logs and assign it to the appropriate application team. This eliminates the need for manual ticket creation, reducing response time and ensuring that the issue is addressed promptly. By streamlining the incident reporting process, AI agents improve efficiency and enhance collaboration between teams handling API-related issues.Additionally, AI agents can provide intelligent recommendations for resolving errors or incidents based on knowledge base articles and past resolutions of similar issues. By leveraging historical data and predefined solutions, AI-driven recommendations can help engineers quickly diagnose and fix problems, significantly reducing the mean time to resolution (MTTR). This proactive approach not only minimizes downtime but also empowers teams to resolve incidents more efficiently, improving overall system reliability and service quality.

Performance Optimization:

Agentic AI can be leveraged to deploy an AI agent that continuously monitors real-time traffic metrics, ensuring optimal API performance and stability. By analyzing incoming request patterns, the agent can detect anomalies, predict potential bottlenecks, and proactively adjust configurations to maintain seamless service availability. This automation reduces the need for manual intervention and enhances overall system efficiency.

One of the key areas where the AI agent can contribute is in fine-tuning API configurations dynamically. This includes adjusting rate-limiting policies based on traffic trends, optimizing CPU and memory allocation, and scaling worker instances to handle fluctuating workloads. By making real-time adjustments, the AI agent helps prevent over utilization, minimizes latency, and ensures APIs operate at peak efficiency, even under varying load conditions.

Co-worker for developers:

Agentic AI can be effectively utilized to expose knowledge base (KB) articles, standards, and guidelines through an interactive chatbot. This AI-driven chatbot can serve as an on-demand resource for developers, allowing them to quickly retrieve relevant information without having to manually search through documentation. By providing instant responses to queries, the chatbot streamlines access to critical technical knowledge, ensuring that developers can focus on coding rather than spending time searching for answers.

This implementation significantly enhances developer efficiency by reducing downtime and eliminating the need for extensive manual research. Developers can ask specific questions related to coding best practices, API usage, or troubleshooting issues, and receive precise guidance based on predefined standards and historical solutions. By integrating this AI-powered chatbot into the development workflow, organizations can foster a more productive and self-sufficient engineering team while ensuring compliance with established guidelines.

Ticket SLA monitoring:

When an incident occurs in production, it can be categorized into different priority levels such as Priority 1, Priority 2, or Priority 3. Each of these categories has its own urgency and corresponding resolution time as per the defined Service Level Agreements (SLA). If an SLA is breached, it can lead to financial penalties for the support engineering team. Therefore, it is crucial to monitor these incidents effectively and ensure timely resolution to avoid any negative business impact.

AI agents can play a significant role in managing SLAs by continuously monitoring their status and sending timely reminders to support engineers. These agents can track the progress of incident resolution, ensuring that deadlines are met. Additionally, AI can take real-time inputs from support engineers, update the incident ticket accordingly, and provide proactive suggestions to accelerate resolution. By automating these tasks, AI reduces the risk of SLA breaches and enhances the efficiency of incident management processes.

AIOps - To Address Observability Challenges

Leading observability and monitoring platforms like IBM, Dynatrace, Elastic, and Datadog have evolved to offer AI-powered solutions under the umbrella of AIOps, bringing intelligence and automation to modern IT operations.

AIOps refers to the use of artificial intelligence and machine learning technologies to enhance and automate various aspects of IT operations. It empowers IT teams to monitor complex systems, detect anomalies, and resolve incidents faster by analyzing vast volumes of operational data in real-time. Traditional monitoring tools often generate thousands of alerts, many of which are false positives or irrelevant. AIOps filters through this noise by correlating data from multiple sources (logs, metrics, events) and surfacing only actionable insights. This helps teams proactively address issues, improve uptime, and optimize performance across distributed system.

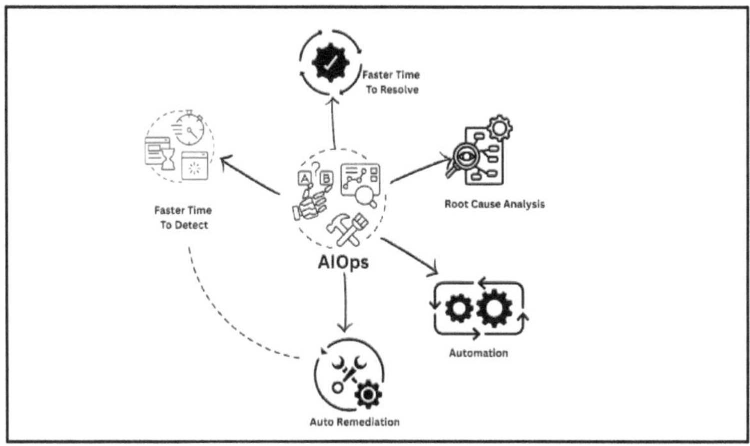

Figure 7.1 - AIOps

Beyond incident detection, AIOps supports predictive analytics, enabling teams to anticipate outages or bottlenecks before they impact users. It plays a vital role in dynamic environments like cloud-native architectures, APIs, and hybrid integration landscapes, where manual monitoring and rule-based alerts fall short. By automating routine tasks such as root cause analysis, ticket creation, and remediation, AIOps reduces the operational burden on DevOps and SRE teams, allowing them to focus on innovation and strategic initiatives. As organizations embrace digital transformation, AIOps becomes a critical pillar for achieving operational resilience and agility.

How AIOps Helps in API Monitoring?

1. Real-Time Anomaly Detection

AIOps uses machine learning to establish baselines for API metrics like response time, error rate, latency, and throughput. When it detects deviations (e.g., sudden spike in 500 errors or slow responses), it flags anomalies immediately — even before SLAs are breached.

Example: Detecting a 15% increase in response time from a specific region that wouldn't be caught by static thresholds.

2. Root Cause Analysis (RCA)

Instead of sifting through thousands of logs, AIOps correlates events across services, infrastructure, and dependencies to identify the root cause of an API failure.

Example: API failures traced back to a slow downstream DB or an expired token — all surfaced automatically.

3. Smart Alerting & Noise Reduction

Traditional monitoring tools often cause alert fatigue. AIOps de-duplicates, correlates, and prioritizes alerts, so teams only get actionable, high-context notifications.

Example: Instead of 50 alerts for failed API calls, you get 1 alert with root cause and impacted APIs/Applications.

4. Predictive Insights

AIOps can predict outages or slowdowns by analyzing historical patterns and usage trends.

Example: It might warn you that your API is likely to hit rate limits next week based on current growth.

5. Automated Remediation

AIOps platforms often integrate with automation tools to trigger self-healing actions, such as restarting APIs/Applications, scaling infrastructure, or updating API keys.

Example: Automatically regenerating a token if an API authentication issue is detected.

6. End-to-End Observability

By integrating logs, metrics, traces, and events, AIOps offers a complete 360° view of API health, performance, and dependencies — critical in API led integration or Hybrid Integration environments.

How AIOps is implemented for API Monitoring?

Let's see how can we implement AIOps for MuleSoft API observability.

Define goals & Use Cases - First thing first, you must identify the pain points and business goals for AIOps.

- What issues do you want to solve? (e.g., alert fatigue, slow RCA)
- What metrics matter most? (e.g., uptime, MTTD/MTTR, SLA compliance)
- Which use cases to start with? (e.g., log analysis, API monitoring, predictive alerting)

Audit and Prepare Your Data - AIOps is only as powerful as the data it gets. Assess and consolidate your observability stack:

- Logs (e.g., from CloudWatch, Splunk, ELK)
- Metrics (e.g., Anypoint Platform Monitoring APIs)
- Events & Alerts (e.g., OpsGenie, PagerDuty)

Choose an AIOps Platform or Toolset - Select a platform that fits your tech stack and maturity level. AIOps Platfrom consist of Machine Learning Models, Different Algorithms. Popular AIOps tools:

- Dynatrace, Datadog, New Relic, IBM – Full-stack observability with AI

- Moogsoft, BigPanda, Splunk ITSI – Event correlation & noise reduction
- Open-source options: Prometheus + Grafana + custom ML, Elastic Stack + ML

Integrate and Ingest Data - Ingest API/Application Logs and metrics to the AIOps platform. We have explained about log data ingestion in Chapter 4, under External Monitoring Tools.

Train Models & Build Baselines - Let the platform learn from historical data to build normal behavior baselines. AIOps tools will detect trends, identify i, spot early warning signals. Some tools use pre-trained models, others need fine-tuning or manual setup.

Enable Correlation & Contextualization - Use the platform to group related events, enrich alerts with context, and trace dependencies across systems (Applications, APIs, Infrastructure). This means filtering out 2-3 meaningful, correlated incidents with root cause hints from1,000 noisy alerts.

Automate Incident Response - Once we are confident in accuracy of the result. Create playbooks for common issues (e.g., restart APIs, call anypoint platform to increase memory, CPU, update timout values, create incident)

Monitor, Fine-Tune & Expand - Review outcome precision and false positive cases. Refine thresholds and model accuracy.

8. Real World Use Cases

Use Case 01: Identifying Dependent APIs in a Growing Application Network

Probelm Statement:

As your organization's API and Application network expands, it becomes increasingly important to track dependencies, especially for highly reusable APIs. A common challenge arises when a System API is consumed by multiple Process and Experience APIs, making it essential to identify which APIs rely on it. Without a clear view of these dependencies, managing updates, troubleshooting issues, and optimizing performance can become complex.

Solution:

To address this, Anypoint Platform offers a Built-in Dashboard for monitoring API dependencies. If your organization is a Titanium Customer, you can leverage the Application Network Dashboard to visualize the relationships between APIs. This feature helps you identify dependent APIs efficiently. However, it is important to note that the dashboard only displays dependencies for APIs that have been actively used within the last 7 days. This ensures that the insights provided are relevant and up-to-date, helping teams make informed decisions about API management and optimization.

Use Case 02: Generating and Analyzing Functional Data as Metrics

Probelm Statement:

The Built-in Dashboard and Custom Dashboard in Anypoint Platform provide insightful charts to analyze various performance-related metrics, such as response times, error rates, and traffic patterns. However, these dashboards primarily focus on technical performance data rather than functional insights, which are essential for understanding business-specific trends within APIs and applications. To make data-driven decisions, organizations need the ability to generate and analyze functional data as metrics, such as the number of successful transactions, customer interactions, or specific business events. For organizations with a Titanium subscription, the Built-in Dashboard offers a Custom Metrics feature, which allows teams to collect and visualize functional data.

Solution:

To achieve this, developers need to integrate a custom connector within the API or application code to capture the relevant functional data and send it to the dashboard as a metric. This enables real-time monitoring of business-specific trends alongside traditional performance metrics. For detailed implementation guidance, refer to the Built-in Dashboard section in this book.

Use Case 03: Unified Monitoring for Transaction Traceability

Problem Statement:

Businesses often require a comprehensive monitoring solution to ensure full traceability of transactions across their systems. This involves the ability to track and analyze logs from the source system, APIs, and target system in a centralized manner. Without such visibility, troubleshooting failures, detecting anomalies, and ensuring seamless data flow between integrated applications can become challenging. A unified monitoring approach helps organizations gain end-to-end insights into transaction flows, enabling proactive issue resolution and improved system reliability.

Solution:

This can be achieved by leveraging external monitoring tools that consolidate logs from APIs and peripheral systems into a centralized observability platform. By ingesting logs into solutions such as Splunk, ELK (Elasticsearch, Logstash, Kibana), or AWS CloudWatch, businesses can efficiently correlate events, analyze trends, and detect anomalies in real time. These tools provide powerful search, filtering, and visualization capabilities, allowing teams to monitor and troubleshoot transactions seamlessly across the entire application ecosystem.

Use Case 04: Implementing Functional Metrics Dashboard Without External Tools

Problem Statement:

With a Titanium Tier subscription, your organization has the capability to design a dashboard for functional metrics, enabling business teams to analyze critical data points. However, if there is no budget allocated for procuring an external monitoring tool, an alternative approach is required. Instead of relying on third-party solutions, your team needs to leverage existing Anypoint Platform capabilities to capture and visualize functional metrics effectively.

Solution:

To achieve this, you can utilize the Custom Metrics Connector to send functional data directly to Anypoint Monitoring. This allows key business metrics to be presented in the Built-in Dashboard, providing a cost-effective and integrated monitoring solution within the MuleSoft Anypoint Monitoring Component. By leveraging this approach, organizations can gain valuable functional insights without additional investment in external tools. For implementation details, refer to the Built-in Dashboard section in Anypoint Monitoring.

Use Case 05: Alerting for High API Traffic

Problem Statement:

In certain scenarios, it is crucial to monitor API traffic spikes to ensure system stability and prevent potential performance degradation. For a specific API, there is a requirement that whenever the traffic exceeds 1,000 requests per minute, the operations team must be notified. Without an automated alerting mechanism, detecting and responding to sudden traffic surges can be challenging, potentially leading to downtime or degraded user experience.

Solution:

This requirement can be addressed using multiple approaches. One effective method is to set up a Rate Limit Alert that triggers a notification when the API traffic surpasses the defined threshold. Additionally, a Policy Violation Alert can be configured for the Rate Limit Policy, ensuring that any unexpected traffic surge is flagged immediately. These proactive monitoring measures help the operations team take timely action, ensuring optimal API performance and system reliability.

Use Case 06: Preventing Recursive Attacks and Data Swings in APIs

Problem Statement:

In a production environment, RESTful APIs are vulnerable to attacks that exploit recursive techniques to consume excessive memory resources or cause unexpected fluctuations in application data size. Such attacks can degrade API performance, leading to high latency, memory exhaustion, or even system crashes. To mitigate these risks, it is essential to implement a solution that monitors API payloads and alerts the support team when anomalous patterns are detected.

Solution:

The first step in designing a robust solution is to analyze the payload structure of each API and establish optimum thresholds for key parameters such as JSON container depth, object entry count, object name length, array element count, and element value length. By defining these constraints at the individual API level, organizations can proactively prevent excessive resource consumption and ensure APIs handle requests within expected limits. The similar configuration can be done for APIs handing XML message. There we can setup XML threat protection policy. Additionally, a policy violation alert should be configured to detect instances where these thresholds are exceeded. By setting up an automated notification system, the support team can be alerted when a specified number of violations occur within a defined time frame. This proactive approach helps safeguard APIs from recursive attacks and abnormal data spikes, ensuring system stability, optimal resource utilization, and enhanced security.

Use Case 07: Ensuring High Availability of Telecom APIs

Problem Statement:

A telecom company relies on APIs to manage critical operations such as customer subscriptions, billing, and service activations. Frequent API downtime can lead to failed transactions, disrupted services, and customer dissatisfaction, ultimately impacting revenue and brand reputation. To prevent these issues, the company needs a proactive monitoring solution that detects API failures in real-time and enables rapid recovery before customers are affected.

Solution:

To achieve this, automated alerts should be configured to immediately notify engineers via email, Slack, or SMS whenever an API becomes unresponsive. Additionally, self-healing mechanisms should be implemented to automatically restart APIs when an outage is detected, minimizing downtime and reducing the need for manual intervention. By integrating these proactive measures, the telecom company can ensure high availability, seamless customer experience, and improved operational efficiency.

Use Case 08: Optimizing API Performance for Real-Time Stock Trading

Problem Statement:

A financial services company provides APIs for real-time stock trading, where even milliseconds of delay can lead to significant financial losses for traders. Slow response times can result in delayed trade executions, negatively impacting user experience and overall market performance. To ensure seamless and high-speed API interactions, the company must implement performance optimization strategies that minimize latency and prevent system overload.

Solution:

To address this, response caching should be implemented at the API Gateway level to reduce redundant computations and accelerate data retrieval. Additionally, throttling techniques should be used to prevent APIs from being overwhelmed by excessive requests, ensuring stable performance during peak trading hours. Monitoring tools such as New Relic, AppDynamics, or OpenTelemetry can be integrated to track response times in real-time, identify performance bottlenecks, and enable proactive issue resolution. These optimizations will help maintain high-speed API performance, ensuring a seamless trading experience for users.

Use Case 09: Preventing Data Breaches in an E-Commerce API

Problem Statement:

An e-commerce platform relies on APIs for handling customer payments, order processing, and inventory management. However, unauthorized access attempts and suspicious API requests have been detected, posing a risk of data breaches and fraud.

Solution:

This can be achieved by implementing API security policies such as OAuth 2.0, rate limiting, and IP whitelisting to restrict unauthorized access. Use real-time monitoring and security analytics to track anomalous traffic patterns. Set up alerts for failed authentication attempts and integrate with SIEM (Security

Information and Event Management) tools for proactive threat detection.

Use Case 10: Ensuring Uptime for a Ride-Sharing API

Problem Statement:

A ride-sharing service provides APIs to connect riders with drivers. However, intermittent API failures result in failed ride bookings and poor user experience. The company needs a high-availability solution to prevent disruptions.

Solution:

This can be achieved by implementing auto-scaling to handle traffic surges during peak hours. Use load balancing to distribute requests across multiple servers. Configure API health checks and automated failover mechanisms to switch to backup instances if a primary API becomes unavailable.

Use Case 11: Reducing Latency in a Healthcare API

Problem Statement:

A healthcare provider uses APIs to retrieve patient records and process insurance claims. However, slow response times lead to delays in accessing critical medical data, affecting doctors and patients.

Solution:

Optimize API performance by implementing edge caching for frequently accessed data. Reduce database query load by implementing indexing and query optimization. Use Asynchronous API processing for non-urgent requests and deploy APM (Application Performance Monitoring) tools to identify bottlenecks.

Use Case 12: Preventing API Abuse in a Streaming Service

Problem Statement:

A video streaming platform provides APIs for content recommendations and user authentication. However, excessive API requests from bots and scrapers are draining system resources and causing performance degradation.

Solution:

This can be solved by using rate limiting and throttling policies to control excessive requests. Implement API key-based authentication and anomaly detection to identify and block suspicious traffic. Leverage bot mitigation techniques to prevent API abuse while ensuring legitimate users are unaffected.

Use Case 13: Error Filtering, Alert Generation & Notification in AWS CloudWatch

Problem Statement:

A company uses MuleSoft for hosting its APIs and Applications. The DevOps team relies on AWS CloudWatch to monitor logs and identify critical errors. However, they are overwhelmed with thousands of log entries, making it difficult to pinpoint and respond to high-priority errors in real time.

Solution:

CloudWatch can be filtered for priority and critical errors and SNS can be used to call a Lambda funtion. This Lambda function can send notificaiton to various notificaiotn channel (Slack, Email etc.). Example of metric filter can be timeout of APIs, 401 access denied calls, OOM Killed error etc.

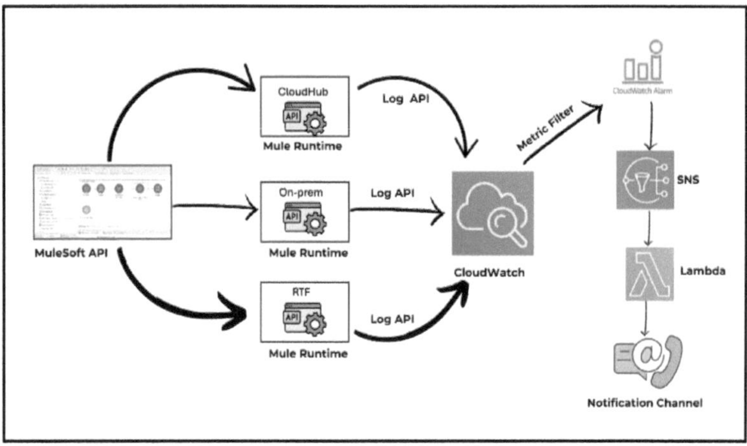

Figure 7.1 - Filtered Error Notification

9. Conclusion

Effective API monitoring is essential for ensuring the performance, reliability, and security of MuleSoft APIs. A well-structured monitoring strategy allows organizations to proactively detect issues, optimize API performance, and maintain seamless integrations. By implementing real-time monitoring, automated alerts, and AI-driven anomaly detection, operations teams can gain deeper visibility into API behavior and take immediate action when needed. These proactive measures help reduce downtime, improve response times, and enhance overall system stability. To maximize the benefits of API monitoring, organizations should leverage comprehensive dashboards that provide real-time insights into API performance, error rates, and traffic patterns. Additionally, integrating API monitoring validation into CI/CD pipelines ensures that APIs consistently comply with performance benchmarks and security standards throughout their lifecycle. This continuous validation approach helps prevent potential failures before deployment, reducing risks and maintaining seamless operations.

As API ecosystems expand, monitoring strategies must evolve to accommodate growing complexities. Regular testing, auditing, and performance optimization are crucial to sustaining API health and delivering a smooth user experience. Best practices such as implementing rate limiting, defining clear error messages, utilising external monitoring tools, and assigning dedicated monitoring roles contribute to building resilient and scalable API infrastructures. These strategies ensure that APIs can efficiently handle increased workloads while maintaining security and compliance. Ultimately, robust API monitoring empowers organizations to drive digital transformation with confidence. By adopting a proactive and adaptive monitoring approach, businesses can ensure that their APIs remain efficient, secure, and highly available, enabling seamless connectivity across systems and enhancing the overall customer experience.

Glossary

IT	Information Technology
API	Application Programming Interface
CICD	Continuous Integration & Continuous Deployment
C4E	Centre for Enablement
SLA	Service Level Agreement
RCA	Root cause analysis
RTF	Runtime Time Fabric
CPU	Central Processing Unit
AWS	Amazon Web Services
SQS	Simple Queue Service
JVM	Java Virtual Machine
VM	Virtual Machine
OS	Operating System
SaaS	Software As A Service
SDLC	Software Development Lifecycle
REST	Representational State Transfer
SOAP	Simple Object Access Protocol

AI	Artificial Intelligence
SR	Service Request
KPI	Key Performance Indicator
NFR	Non Functional Requirement
NRLQ	New Relic Query Language
MTTR	Mean Time To resolution
KB	Knowledge Base
SIEM	Security Information And Event Management
APM	Application Performance Monitoring
MTTD	Mean Time To Detection

References

1. https://docs.mulesoft.com
2. https://docs.newrelic.com
3. https://docs.datadoghq.com
4. https://platform.openai.com/docs/concepts
5. https://www.elastic.co/docs
6. https://anypoint.mulesoft.com/exchange/portals/anypoint-platform
7. https://docs.splunk.com/Documentation
8. https://docs.aws.amazon.com
9. https://www.atlassian.com/software/opsgenie

www.ingramcontent.com/pod-product-compliance
Ingram Content Group UK Ltd.
Pitfield, Milton Keynes, MK11 3LW, UK
UKHW042020190726
13854UKWH00005B/2381